Missed

Hard of Hearing in

Connections

a Hearing World

Barbara Stenross

 Temple University Press
PHILADELPHIA

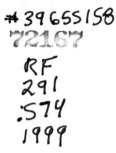
Temple University Press, Philadelphia 19122
Copyright © 1999 by Temple University
All rights reserved
Published 1999
Printed in the United States of America

∞ The paper used in this publication meets the requirements of
the American National Standard for Information Sciences—Permanence
of Paper for Printed Library Materials, ANSI Z39.48–1984

Library of Congress Cataloging-in-Publication Data

Stenross, Barbara, 1946–
    Missed Connections : hard of hearing in a hearing world / Barbara Stenross.
        p.   cm.
    Includes bibliographical references and index.
    ISBN 1-56639-681-6 (alk. paper). — ISBN 1-56639-682-4 (pbk. : alk. paper)
    1. Stenross, Barbara, 1946–   2. Hearing impaired—United States—
Biography.   I. Title.
RF291.S74   1999
362.1'978'092—dc21
    [b]   98-30716
                                                                    CIP

For My Father

Contents

List of Figures

Acknowledgments

When I attended my first meeting of Village Self Help for Hard of Hearing People (Village SHHH) in 1991, I understood hearing loss only as something I wanted to learn more about as a sociologist and daughter. Today, with a hearing loss of my own, I know firsthand the potential for disconnection that is borne in mishearing and bred by silence. But from SHHH meetings I also know that the collective wisdom of others can help. No one must face this journey alone.

I have many people to thank for help with this book. First are the men and women of Village SHHH. You are the experts whose experience and courage inform all its pages; whose compassion and laughter have carried it forward.

I thank the founders of and subscribers to Beyond-Hearing. When I found out about this Internet e-mail list in 1995, I thought I'd subscribe to round out my knowledge. Three years later, I'm still enjoying the information and exchanges on this lively self-help forum. Thank you for allowing me to include selected postings.

Many people have helped with the writing and thinking. At the top of this list are my best friend, Sherryl Kleinman, and the women in my writing group: Marcy Lansman, Sybil Wagner, and Karla Henderson. At our lunchtime discussions and our weekly sessions, you taught me to write in scenes, without academic jargon. I cannot thank you four enough.

For additional help with the writing, I thank Michael Schwalbe, who read the whole manuscript when I could no longer "see" it; Joanne Reeves and Kate Smith, who encouraged me in the early stages; Erica Fox, who did the copyediting; and Barbara Conti, Mary Jane Silvey, and Carolyn Allen, who provided a booster shot of advice and encouragement near the end of the writing process.

For his trust and support, I thank Editor-in-Chief Michael Ames. You skillfully guided the manuscript from its ethnographic beginnings to its self-help conclusion.

I thank Dr. Samuel Trychin. Readers will benefit greatly from your allowing me to quote extensively from your psychology workshop.

I thank a long list of friends and colleagues. At critical moments, each of you generously interrupted your own work to share your knowledge and answer my questions. From the beginning, Joan Black, John Black, Dorothy Allen, Betty Beckerman, and Lucy Straley; later, Melody Harrison, Jackie Jaloszynski, Mark Haythorn, Stiles Stribling, Wade Alston, Ruth Miller, Carl Viehe, Carole Williamson, Roberta Hedrick, Ruth Livingston, Jim Kessler, Shirin Kaye-Sacek, Margaret Rothschild, Lamia Via, Najiye Weslow, Deborah Szafron, Susan Foster, Nancy Ferguson, and an anonymous reviewer.

I thank my brother, Frederick Matthew Stenross. Your memories helped me understand and write about our father better.

Last, but not least, I thank my beloved husband, Majid, and our son, Adam. You helped me keep things in perspective.

Carrboro, North Carolina
July 1998

Introduction

One week after Mom's funeral, I was eating breakfast in the kitchen of the house I grew up in, suitcase ready at the door for the afternoon trip to the airport. Between bites of cereal, I heard Dad fiddling with something in the living room. Then three sharp claps. More fiddling, then more claps. "Damn."

I joined him. "What's wrong?"

"This hearing aid's not working." Dad sat down on the couch, removed his hearing aid, changed the battery, put the aid back in his ear, then clapped his hands to see if he could hear himself.

"Damn." Dad frowned, then got up quickly and crossed the room.

"Where are you going?"

"Downtown, to have this looked at. To the hearing aid place."

"I'll drive," I said, and grabbed the keys from the kitchen shelf.

On the drive downtown, Dad didn't hear me. I turned my head and raised my voice. "Which exit is it?"

Again, he didn't understand.

"15B or 15C?" Just as we were about to miss it, Dad waved me onto 15B.

The hearing aid dealer had three simple rooms in an old office building. At nine in the morning, we were the only customers. The fitter took Dad's hearing aid into the next room. A few minutes later he had it working again.

"Don't wait so long the next time. It needed cleaning," the man said.

Turning to me, he whispered, "He hasn't been able to hear for weeks."

I took a step back. Had Dad understood Mom's words from her hospital bed? What about the visitation, funeral, lawyer, grandchildren—how much had he missed?

Dad took out his wallet to pay, but the man waved it away. As he opened the door into the hallway for us, he slapped Dad lightly on the back.

"You're a new man now," he said, and laughed.

Dad had worn a hearing aid for fifteen years but had let it go without fixing it for weeks. Now Mom wasn't there to do his calling and listening for him. When friends and neighbors stopped by to talk, he would have to hold up his end of the conversation. On the day that I was scheduled to leave, Dad realized it was time to fix his hearing aid.

Dad lost partial hearing in one ear during World War II, while serving in the U.S. Army in Europe. Yet throughout my childhood and into my early teens, I was mostly unaware of his hearing problem. Each month when his small veteran's benefit check arrived in the mail—compensation for his hearing disability—he put it aside for Christmas presents. Dad never quite trusted medical diagnoses or doctors. He denied the need for a hearing aid.

I began noticing Dad's hearing loss more often when I came home from college. Each summer vacation, the TV was louder. When I lived at home to work and save money during my final semester, I hated being home in the evenings. As I went upstairs to my bedroom to study, I closed all the doors between me and the blaring TV.

Later, I would be reminded of Dad's hearing loss during our occasional visits. I had always thought of Dad as quiet. Now, he seemed quieter still. Then Mom began complaining about miscommunications. She said she told Dad things he later denied she'd said. Mom began pushing Dad to be fitted for a hearing aid, and, at the age of seventy, he finally gave in.

Dad seemed happier and more in touch with people after he got his hearing aid. He played ball with his grandsons and pinochle with friends. Still, the hearing aid didn't remedy Dad's reliance on Mom. She scheduled his appointments and handled the calls.

I reluctantly left Dad on his own when I flew back home to finish out the semester teaching sociology at the University of North Carolina.

Earlier that fall, I had begun looking for a site for a fieldwork project—a place or setting I could study firsthand and in depth, by hanging out, observing interactions, and asking questions. In December, an ad in the newspaper caught my eye: "Village Self Help for Hard of Hearing People (Village SHHH), second Wednesday of the month, community church." I had found the group I wanted to study. Yet, at my first meeting, I introduced myself as the daughter of someone who was hard of hearing.

At that time, Ann, one of the founders of Village SHHH, was serving as the chair of the group. Ann had lost much of her hearing early in life, possibly from a bout of measles when she was two or three. Now in her forties, she and her hearing husband, Tom, had recently opened a business selling and installing communications equipment and visual alerting devices. When I told them about Dad, they understood.

"Most of our customers come in because a spouse has died," Tom said, shaking his head. "They've been depending on the family to call, the husband or wife to do the telephoning and make the appointments. All of a sudden, there is no spouse, and they're in all sorts of trouble."

At Village SHHH, several members were also widowed, but some came as couples—the hard-of-hearing person and the hearing partner.

Although I was eager to learn more about hearing loss, most of that first meeting was spent on organizational matters. Members had been holding meetings for about ten years, but now the chapter was going through internal changes. Ann announced that she could no longer serve as chair; others would have to do more work. Maggie, a retired professor of communications, offered to serve as president. Then, when the recording secretary said she also had to quit, I volunteered to take the minutes.

The next month, as I stood nervously before the assembled members and asked permission to audio-record the interaction and write about the group, a woman named Cora raised her hand for the mike.

"I think it's fine," she said. "We want more people to know what it's like."

"Some people might want to know what happens to the research later," the hearing partner of one man said.

"I can't guarantee that it would have a big impact." I searched for each word carefully. "This kind of research often doesn't lead to changes."

Louisa, a round-faced older woman, quickly spoke up.

"I think it is good if you stay with us even if you don't write," she said, "because that way, we can tell you our frustrations!"

"I am in favor—I move that you do it," a man with a deep voice said.

Nineteen votes for; zero against. As I understood later, members were voting to be heard.

For four years beginning in January 1991, I audiotaped and transcribed the full meetings of each monthly gathering of Village SHHH. Over time, I also interviewed twelve of the self-help group's central members. In these and later informal conversations, members shared more of their histories and personal experiences.

In 1995, I began seeking out information from other sources. On September 17–19, I attended the first state conference for and about hard-of-hearing people, "Breaking Sound Barriers," presented by the North Carolina Division of Services for the Deaf and Hard of Hearing and by the first state SHHH organization, North Carolina Self Help for Hard of Hearing People. I subscribed to Beyond-Hearing, an Internet e-mail list "owned" by Dr. Miriam Clifford and run by Majordomo software at Duke University. And I attended and audiotaped a workshop, "Mental Health and Hard of Hearing," offered by Dr. Samuel Trychin, a former professor of psychology at Gallaudet University and an expert on strategies for coping with hearing loss.

Attending Village SHHH meetings opened a new world for me. From my first meeting, I began to realize that Dad's hearing loss played a bigger role in his life—and in our family—than I had imagined. With each successive gathering, the impact of that reality hit closer to home. Had Mom's loving service contributed to Dad's frequent silence? What could we all have done to better connect?

Once a month, Village SHHH provided a safe and friendly haven for people to discuss their frustrations and ask their questions. Through role plays, interactions with guest speakers, and open-mike discussions, members pooled their experiences and learned from each other.

Some members, like Ann, grew up with a hearing loss; they always knew they had a hearing problem. Others took their ears for granted until one day they noticed that their hearing had changed. No longer could they readily follow conversation. They confronted muffled sounds and missing words.

"It only happened six years ago," Miles, a regular at the meetings, once told the group. "Up to that point I had a mild hearing loss [in my right ear] at high frequencies and a hearing aid that didn't seem—well, that I didn't always wear. But all of a sudden I discovered I couldn't hear on the phone with my left ear, couldn't talk to my wife in bed if I was sleeping on my right side, even though I was looking at her."

Miles's experience was typical of many of the older members of the group. It is a common experience in the United States. Twenty-eight million Americans have hearing loss (Dugan 1997). Among people over the age of sixty-five, hearing loss affects nearly one in three (Gates et al. 1990; Gordon-Salant 1990). Only a tiny fraction can communicate by signing. The rest must bridge frequent gaps in the spoken word.

Missed Connections is the story of how a few missed sounds in conversation can create large gaps in communication. In scenes and dialogues from chapter meetings, Village SHHH members show how it's possible to listen but miss the "connecting words"—the words that bring it all together, the words that give the conversation sense.

But this book also offers a message of hope. Through stories, anecdotes, and information sessions, Village SHHH members share some of the ways they have found to reconnect. If you are hard of hearing or know someone who is, I hope that this book will be useful to you.

A note about names: When I joined Village SHHH, I promised members privacy and confidentiality. Consequently, I use made-up names for chapter members. I use real names for public figures and for a few Beyond-Hearing subscribers who asked me to. Self Help for Hard of Hearing People is the organization's actual title; "Village" is a pseudonym.

1 Missed Connections

We were discussing communication within the family when Julie motioned for the mike. Julie, an office worker in her fifties, seldom came to meetings, but she appeared at this one with her housemate Don. After a glance at him, she plunged ahead.

"I think one of my biggest frustrations is missing the one or two crucial connecting words that let me know what really happened," she said. "I know, for instance, that someone in the house is putting the cats outside for exercise, but what I miss is the one or two words that let me know: Has he taken the cats out for exercise, or is he asking *me* to? And when I ask, 'What did you say?' the words get repeated.

"It's very difficult for people to realize that all you want again are those one or two words. And I hear, 'I'm talking about the cats going out to be exercised,' and I scream back, 'I know that's what you're talking about, but *have* they gone out, are *you* taking them out, or do you want *me* to?'"

Julie laughed, and the others joined in. "And I found out that this is what happens," she said with a nod, "I miss the little connecting *a*s, *and*s, and *but*s, or whatever."

"I think that's a tremendously important point," Walt, a retired financial officer, said. "If anybody figures out how to ask for the connecting word without having to listen to the whole damn thing all over again and missing it again, I'd be happy to know about it!"

A few weeks later, Ann and Tom gave a presentation to the group. "Why do you hear but not understand? Do you?

Is that common?" Ann asked. Heads bobbed up and down around the room.

"This is the first thing that Ann and I had to learn," Tom said. "That you can *hear* but not *understand* the word."

I had to learn that difference, too. When hard-of-hearing people say they've missed a word, they have almost always heard sound. The problem is that the sound lacks meaning—they've missed what makes those sounds "words."

"Your voice is made up of both low- and high-frequency sounds," Tom explained to the chapter members. "You don't speak like a middle C on the piano, in one tone. Most of the vowels are in the low frequencies. Most everyone who's hard of hearing hears vowels—*ahhh, eee.* But as you get up in the frequencies are the consonants, the *t*s, *sh*s, *p*s, *t*s, *P*s, *T*s, *P*s, *T*s." As Tom repeated, he raised his voice for emphasis. "*Those* are the things that are hard to hear. And if you can't hear the consonant, you can't understand the word. That's really why you hear but don't understand the word.

"Ann's hearing loss—even with two hearing aids, what does she miss? She misses the *t*s, the *f*s, the *th*s. She *never* hears them. That is why you hear noise. People are actually speaking outside your ability to hear."

Ann joked about those missing consonants. "'Like a Bridge over Troubled Waters'—I hear 'Like a Pitcher of Water.' And how about, 'I'll Never Be Your Beast of Burden'—'I'll Never Be Your Pizza Burning'!"

Susan stood up to agree. "Whenever they announce the temperature on the TV, I can't tell if it's fifty-six or sixty-six. I have to go look at the thermometer."

In 1995, SHHH national president Julie Olson spoke at the North Carolina conference "Breaking Sound Barriers." Olson got her first hearing aid as an adult. In her talk, she wondered whether her hearing loss began before she started school. "My mother had written down some of my bright sayings in my baby book," Julie said in her afternoon session. "One of them was from when I came home from kindergarten. I had this lovely drawing of a horse, and my teacher added my caption for the picture: 'This is gravity. Gravity is a big horse.' Well," Julie laughed, "the teacher had told us that gravity was a big *force*!

"My mom thought that was the cutest thing, but I wonder, I really wonder, if it was because I didn't hear. That *f* sound, of course, is a very, very soft sound. It's one of the sounds we miss very early when we have a hearing loss."

Later in her presentation, Julie returned to this theme of missed consonants. "When you see a word with only vowels in it, it's very hard to figure out what it is," she said. "The *consonants* are what give sound meaning. I love to do this with spouses of hard-of-hearing people." Julie used a felt-tip pen to write out a pattern of vowels and blanks that appeared on the screen overhead. "Anyone know what this is?"

$$\_\_E\,E\_\quad O\_\quad\_O\_\_U\_E$$

When no one raised a hand, Julie jumped in. "It's 'Wheel of Fortune!'" she grinned. "We're pretty good at that, too, by the way. It's amazing how well we do when we're watching that program!"

The Audiogram

Most hard-of-hearing people miss the high-frequency consonants, but everyone's hearing loss is a little different.

"This is an audiogram," Dr. Melanie Harris, a speech pathologist and professor of speech and hearing sciences, told chapter members during a talk on recent developments in

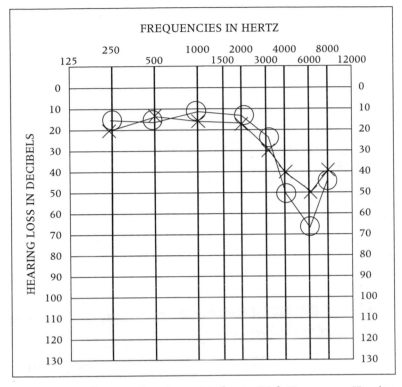

Figure 1. Audiogram showing a Moderate High Frequency Hearing Loss in Both Ears.

hearing aids. "It's a graph of a person's hearing loss." As Dr. Harris spoke, she drew the outlines of an audiogram on a green chalkboard. A reproduction of an actual audiogram is shown in figure 1. Audiograms are used to diagram hearing loss and to fit people with hearing aids.

"Now, this is the loudness scale, along this parameter," Dr. Harris pointed to the vertical axis of the graph. "Zero to 10 [decibels], to me, is normal hearing. To audiologists, zero decibels is where people with normal hearing can just barely detect a tone 50 percent of the time it is presented. It's a threshold. One hundred and ten is jet engines revving up, jackhammers, that sort of thing.

"On the frequency scale, 250 is your San Francisco foghorn sound. And right here"—she pointed to the area around 1,000 to 4,000 Hz—"are some of the speech sounds, like the fricatives, *sh, th*—that's where most of their energy is carried. When people have hearing losses, typically it's a hearing loss something like this: some configuration of better hearing in the lower frequencies, [and] less better as you go higher and higher and higher. What that means is that this speech information that's out here"—Dr. Harris swept her hand over the right side of the audiogram—"is not heard. Without amplification, and even sometimes with it, you just can't—it's *not available* to you."

Months later, when Dr. Harris learned I was writing this book, she suggested I include a figure from *Hearing and Hearing Loss in Children,* a textbook by Jerry Northern and Marion Downs. Reprinted here as figure 2, the diagram shows familiar sounds plotted against a standard audiogram. Figure 2 suggests that the person whose audiogram is shown in figure 1 would have difficulty distinguishing between the "fifty-six" and "sixty-six" in Susan's example.

Although audiograms show response curves at seven or more frequencies or pitches, people sometimes summarize hearing losses in a single figure. One way to do this—remembering that all such summaries sacrifice important information—is to average the decibel loss over three or five frequencies, customarily 500, 1,000, and 2,000 Hz. Using this measure, the hearing loss in figure 1 is 15 decibels, a loss usually labeled "mild." Losses of 60 dB are labeled "severe"; 90 dB, "profound" (Yellin and Roland 1997). Under guidelines established by the American Academy of Otolaryngology and the American Council of Otolaryngology,

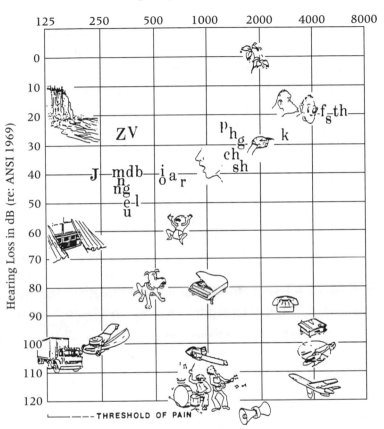

Figure 2. Frequency Spectrum of Familiar Sounds Plotted on Standard Audiogram.

however, a hearing loss of 25 decibels can be disabling enough to qualify a person for industrial compensation (Northern and Downs 1991). Losses as small as 15 decibels can interfere with children's learning of speech (Northern and Downs 1991).

Decibels are measured in a logarithmic, not an arithmetic, scale. Consequently, small numerical differences in decibels reflect huge differences in hearing and the ability to understand speech. For example, 10 decibels is ten times louder than 0 decibels; 20 decibels is one hundred times louder than 10 decibels; and 30 decibels is one thousand times louder than 20 decibels (Pope 1997: 14).

Most members of Village SHHH could quote their hearing loss in decibels. "I'm just about between 65 and 70 decibels, bilaterally, straight across the chart," Delores, one of the early founders of Village SHHH, told me when I interviewed her. "Straight as an arrow across the chart."

"Is that unusual?" I asked. At the time, I'd not yet seen an audiogram. I thought I was studying the "social" dynamics of the group.

"Yes, it is," Delores answered. "Usually you start out hearing the low notes better, and then you start going down, so to have it straight across the chart is unusual. But I'm lucky—it hasn't changed since I was thirty."

Karen said her hearing loss had always been "between 75 and 85 decibels" in both ears. "One hundred [decibels] is like a train horn, something like that," she told me as a benchmark example. "I can hear *that*."

Sarah had a hearing loss that qualified her as legally deaf. "In North Carolina, when they used to do a tax exemption, I always met their criteria for legally deaf," she said. "I have a 90-decibel loss, and then it's a slight slant down, to below 110."

"Can you hear anything without your hearing aids?" I asked.

"If there was a jet plane taking off right next to me, I could probably hear that," Sarah answered, then corrected herself. "I would probably feel the vibrations more than hear the sound. . . . I think people don't realize, because I get along pretty well in terms of communication and how I act with people, that my hearing is worse than it appears."

Most members of Village SHHH were familiar with their audiograms, but Miles knew his like the back of his hand. "I've made some measurements of my own," Miles said one day at a chapter meeting. "The audiologists only measure frequency every so often; they don't do enough detail work to my satisfaction as an engineer. So I got a signal generator and a couple of earphones and I ran my own curves and discovered that I have a big hole all through the voice range in my left ear. The response curve takes a dive at about 300 cycles or Hertz, which is in the men's voice range, but it doesn't get consonants and things, it just gets the basics, so I can hear *womp, womp, womp,* you know, pretty good. But anything from there up to about 2,000 cycles, which is in the consonants, the hissing sounds, and so forth, this ear doesn't hear. It manufactures a hiss out of all the sounds between 300 and about 2,000 cycles."

Miles gave an example of the social consequences of this "consonant" problem. "This happened in the dining room [at my retirement village]," he said. "One of my good friends and neighbors wanted me to sit with her at the table, and I came in the door and I had my eye on somebody else and I was heading in that direction. She told me later, 'Miles, I called you and I called you. I wanted you to come sit with us.' Well, my name is different, but it's not recognizable except when I hear it well. I mean . . . if you knock a few consonants off of Miles, you just—it doesn't sound like anything particular."

Connecting Words

Missed consonants lead to missed words. Missed words can defeat the larger sense.

"You know, we can just miss one word in a sentence, and

that means that the whole context of the sentence is gone," Ann said at one of my first meetings at Village SHHH. I thought I misheard her. How can one word embody the entire context? Don't people use the context of the message, along with the words they do understand, to fill in the blanks and regain the whole?

In fact, although hard-of-hearing people are always trying to "fill in the blanks," they don't always succeed. When that happens, they feel they have missed the word that gives context, the word that *connects*.

Hard-of-hearing people's experience fits with what some researchers have learned about how people create meaning from speech. According to the "reflexivity principle" of talk, each part of a sentence frames, or contexts, all other parts. As ethnomethodologists Hugh Mehan and Houston Wood (1975: 12) put it, "An utterance not only delivers some particular information, it also creates a world in which information itself can appear." From this perspective, each word helps build the house; one missed word can bring the house down.

A hard-of-hearing person can experience such a collapse at any moment: watching TV with their partners, talking to their doctors, sharing conversation with friends. One minute they're following; the next, they're lost. If the conversation is straightforward and they know the subject, the redundancy of conversation (Wardhaugh 1993: 106–7) may enable them to get the gist. They miss out the most when conversation takes an unexpected turn—a speaker's first words, or a change in topic. They also miss the twists and surprises that make up humor.

"In my whole hearing loss period, I don't think I've ever gotten the punch line of anybody's joke," Ron, a retired businessman, said, reflecting a theme that came up again and again among chapter members. "People get to the punch line, then they lower their voices."

"I still get left out," Karen said, "and I get left out of the punch line, and that really hurts."

Louisa sighed, "I haven't heard a joke since I don't know when."

"I *never* get the punch line," Jan, a retired teacher, told me when we spoke together in her apartment. "In a conversation, if you get four or five words out of ten, and you know something about what is being discussed, you can follow it. But the punch line is always a surprise."

As Jan noted, punch lines mark a shift in a conversation. They're humorous because they take a story in a new direction. Hard-of-hearing people experience sudden shifts all the time, but when the speaker doesn't intend them.

Missing a punch line can disconnect in a more painful way. Jokes often serve as cultural "understanding tests" (Sacks 1974: 346). When hard-of-hearing people miss a punch line, they may feel excluded from the social circle. They see that the unintelligible words carried something magic and funny because others are laughing, or the speaker wants them to and they cannot—at least not, as Jan put it, "with any real mirth." Asking for a repeat can disrupt the occasion. Even if they "get it," they know they missed the original moment and the union that occurred when the shift in conversation resulted in laughter.

Maybe it is because laughter is so important to human connection that members turned mishearing into punch lines when they told jokes.

"This fellow told his friend he got a new hearing aid," Fred smiled, as he began a joke.

"'Oh,' the friend said, 'What kind is it?'"

Fred looked at his wrist. "'Two o'clock.'"

On the day Ann and Tom discussed the sounds of hearing loss, Ann put a transparency of a comic strip up on the screen. "I hope you can see this little cartoon here," Ann said. "It's something that I think is very common to all of us. In the first frame, a woman knocks at her neighbor's door. 'Good morning,' she says to the man who opens it. 'I'd like you to come share my warm bread.' He follows her home. 'Uh-oh,' he thinks, as she invites him to sit at her kitchen table. 'I thought she said share her warm bed!'"

The comic strip went on for a few more frames. At the end of it, Ann looked around at the group. "I thought that was a wonderful cartoon because it's just the thing that can happen to us. We can mess up with just one little word, one little *sh* or *th*."

"What *is* hearing loss?" Ann asked. "What does it really mean?"

Ann paused a moment before she answered. "It's a major life loss. It isn't fatal and it's not painful, but it *is* a major loss. When a person is hard of hearing, the ability to communicate with others is out of order."

No matter how hard they work at listening, hard-of-hearing people will always miss some sounds. When this happens, they can miss a conversation's *a*s, *and*s, and *but*s. They risk the loss of *connecting words*.

2 Belonging and Acceptance

"I love this group," Karen said one Saturday morning as we were passing the microphone around for introductions. "I wish we could have more meetings." For many members, Village SHHH was the one place where they could expect to hear and be heard in a gathering or group.

In encounters with more than two or three others, hard-of-hearing people often feel lost. They can't hear one person over the others and the background noise, can't tell whether a speaker has completed her turn or has only paused for breath. Should they butt in? Stay quiet? Grab the floor? Make their exit? Members had tried all these strategies; none felt like the right solution.

"One problem I have in particular," Fred told the other members, "is being unable to join in conversation for fear that I haven't heard what someone said, or if I'm going to be saying something that doesn't need to be said at that point— I just don't know. And so I end up by sometimes saying nothing, and I don't get much out of the meeting then."

Walt identified with Fred's experience. "I've had times where I thought the person was done talking but they weren't, and they let me know. Now I sometimes won't say anything for an hour, an hour and a half. . . . We went out to dinner the other night; it was someone's birthday. I might as well have taken along a magazine."

The SHHH Model

At Village SHHH, we used several strategies to ensure that everyone felt included in the group. We sat in a circle, took turns speaking, and used a sound field (PA) system, a microphone, and an audio loop.

We also searched out appropriate spaces for our meetings. For example, when the community church moved us to a room without carpeting or curtains, Maggie looked for a new location. At the village center—our next home—we also asked to be moved twice. The fluorescent lights in the first room interfered with the telecoils in some members' hearing aids, destroying the reception within the audio loop. The next location was near a corridor, catching the noise of center traffic. Today we meet in a corner room with absorbent carpeting and good light. We push card tables together to accommodate the number of people present. Seated across from each other around these tables, we can all see each other's faces.

At our meetings, members also took time to instruct each other. For example, Maggie taught me to hold the microphone close to, but not so it covered, my mouth. At first, I held it too low or gestured with it. Even Ann, our most knowledgeable member, occasionally received coaching when she spoke. Almost as soon as Ann began one day, for example, Ed raised his hand for the mike. "Can you speak more slowly," he asked her.

Ann looked confused, then pretended to frown. "Speak . . . slowly," she drawled, "and distinctly," she quipped, panning the group with a big grin.

Village SHHH meetings provided not only a model for group communication but also a time and place to talk about it. On two occasions, for example, we role-played ways to improve our experiences in restaurants: Ask for a round table, if possible, and in a corner or against a wall—avoid the middle of the room or near the kitchen; set the candle to the side; sit in good lighting; study the menu and the salad dressings before the server arrives; ask the server to list the specials in writing.

We also discussed—and sometimes examined—portable technologies members could take with them to other groups. For example, Sarah brought in her assistive listening kit. Among the modules was a directional mike she could place on a table or hold out in front. More recently, an audiologist told us that some hearing aids come with directional mikes as a built-in option.

But what drew most members back to our meetings again and again was the chance to be with others who understood. Since other people had problems but found ways to cope, losing hearing didn't have to be the end of the world.

"What SHHH tries to do," SHHH, Inc., founder Howard E. "Rocky" Stone explained at a banquet in his honor in December 1992, "is to help you understand some of the things that are happening to you, to get them into perspective, make you more aware of the possibilities that exist, and start developing a relationship with yourself and with other people. Change is a lot easier when you're surrounded by friendly people who themselves are changing, and who are encouraging you."

At the 1992 banquet, Rocky Stone presented an award to one of our chapter members. In her late sixties, Delores had, with Ann and Tom and others, helped co-found our Village chapter. A few months earlier, when I asked Delores how SHHH had helped her, she replied, "I guess because I'm with people who are hard of hearing and we're all in the same boat. This is what I was acutely aware of at the first [national] convention I went to, the first SHHH convention. It was in '84 in Chicago, there were only three hundred people there, but I was just immediately aware at that first gathering that evening—everybody else, nobody else hears well. It doesn't matter if I have to ask them to repeat. They're going to ask me to repeat, too."

Delores paused for a moment, then continued more slowly. "Being a member of SHHH certainly gave me much more self-esteem. At that time, I was newly widowed, and I just needed a boost. I was shy to begin with, and hearing loss had made me feel less worthy."

Delores was the second person I interviewed. Partway through our conversation, she corrected me gently when I referred to our chapter as Village "Shush."

"Ah, by the way," Delores said, "I don't think you call it Shush. You have to say, spell it out—*S, H, H, H.* Even Rocky sometimes only gets two of the *H*s."

"Sometimes I've heard four," I said, and we laughed.

Why were the initials so important? Although newcomers sometimes called the organization Shush or Shhhh, seasoned members like Delores always gave the full name or spelled it out. I think it was because they didn't want to diminish the organization or its members in any way, or to suggest any connotations of staying quiet. They saw SHHH as encouraging people to speak out.

At a meeting almost two years later, Delores also reminded us that "hard of hearing" doesn't follow *the* but modifies *people.*

"I just have one comment about one word someone said here," Delores said. "They said Self Help for *the* Hard of Hearing. Now, if you say Self Help for *the* Hard of Hearing, you are putting us in a category. But we're Self Help for Hard of Hearing *People.* We're part of the *world.*"

At Village SHHH meetings, members were reminded that they were people first and hard of hearing second (Stone 1990: 42). By meeting with others who understood, they moved from isolation and withdrawal to belonging and acceptance.

National Organization

Members who attended national meetings moved toward acceptance even faster.

"What's nice about going to the conventions," Sarah reported back to the group after her first SHHH, Inc., convention, "is, in our small organization and our workplace or whatever, I think a lot of times we get the feeling we're the only one with these problems. But if you go to the national organization, you think, 'My God, everybody else is like me!'

"So what's really nice about it is the sense of community, sharing, going to workshops, trying to get more information on becoming better advocates for what you need. I grew up with a hearing loss, so it's been good to have that contact. It makes me a little emotional. Ohhhh." Sarah smiled, but her eyes filled with tears.

"One thing I want to mention," Karen piped up, "is, the reason I go to the conventions is to socialize! . . . They have a lot of social activities geared to the young adult. I think the SHHH organization has helped me more than anything else. It's brought me more friends."

In high school, Karen rarely participated in clubs or went to large gatherings. "Mostly, I think I was alone," she told me when I talked to her in her parents' living room. "I mean, I was very alone. I didn't talk much in class. I didn't raise my hand in class. Most of my friendships were one-on-one. . . . I never went to any of the parties or social functions after school because it was always too dark. I went to one party, like a spring fling, and I didn't like it at all. I went in there and it was dark, and I couldn't see anything so I couldn't hear anything. I think I got one of my friend's mothers to take me home."

In her junior year, hoping to get more involved in social activities, Karen switched to a residential school for the deaf. As one of a handful of students who wore a hearing aid, she was still on the outside, looking in.

"I had a hard time learning signs," Karen began. "Well, not so much a hard time, it was just—it was hard for them to accept me. It took me almost to the end of that year to be accepted by the Deaf students. . . . I took my hearing aids off one day in class and the teacher said, 'Karen, you put those hearing aids back on!' (Laugh.) I said, 'Well, I was seeing how it was to be like the other kids for a change.'"

In 1988, at her first SHHH convention, Karen finally fit in. "I was really bubbly, I was so tickled about it. Everybody else was like I was. Everything was closed-captioned; all the workshops were closed-captioned. But the best thing was the social activities. I think I had more fun in the social activities that year than all my other years before put together, if you know what I mean. It's the one place I date," she winked.

"They're wonderful, aren't they," Ann agreed. "All those hearing aids! Everybody has hearing aids! It's perfect. Everybody's so relaxed about it, and they enjoy themselves. It's a whole different ballgame."

For Ann, SHHH conventions functioned as annual homecomings and a kind of home base—inspiring her to try other meetings and groups.

"With the SHHH meetings, the national ones, I learned about the different ways of doing things," Ann told me in her interview. "I saw different people, how they coped. I did know that we all said we had never met any other hard-of-hearing people before. That, and being on the national board, was really something that changed everything. I was suddenly having to speak up, and I had never done that before. And then I went to Toastmasters because I thought, 'Geez, I'm going to have to learn to speak up, and I don't know how to do this.' So, I was learning. That was a very crucial part of my getting out in the world."

Chapter members who attended the national conventions drew closer from the experience. Their hearing problems brought them together rather than pushed them apart. Yet convention goers were the exception to the rule in our local chapter. Most Village SHHH members had lost hearing as older adults. Although they welcomed the instant acceptance and camaraderie of chapter meetings, they relied for sociability on old memberships and affiliations in the hearing world. Yet, even for these members, Village SHHH had an important function. By meeting others who had hearing loss, they moved more quickly toward accepting that "loss" and also more quickly toward accepting themselves.

Dana Mulvany, a founder of the Beyond-Hearing Internet e-mail list, suggested that groups like SHHH may be crucial to this acceptance process. "I think one of the reasons why SHHH, ALDA [Association of Late Deafened Adults], and other organizations of people with hearing loss and other disabilities are so important," Dana wrote, "is because they at least indirectly help counter the negative attitudes about hearing loss present in other social environments. As we meet other people with hearing loss, we are able to look beyond their hearing loss to appreciate who they are. As we accept their needs, we come to accept our own."

3 Hearing Aids and Lipreading

Hearing Aids

Like many newcomers to Village SHHH, Kate had recently learned that she had a hearing loss. She wanted advice on hearing aids.

"What are your main resources for deciding on the right kind of hearing aid?" she asked the group.

"That's a tricky one," Miles answered, "because some dealers don't represent more than one company, so if you need a hearing aid, yes, they'll fit you, and there's any number of those around, but they'll sell you the one that they represent."

"Go to an audiologist," Sarah, a teacher and the current president, said. "One thing you shouldn't do is go to a hearing aid dealer to get tested. Go to an audiologist. Too, make sure you get at least a thirty-day, one-month time to try it, because, if it doesn't work and you don't like it, you can bring it back."

Sarah had a lot of experience with hearing aids. She had gotten her first hearing aid when she was six. Sarah went on to recommend an audiologist she liked. "She dispenses hearing aids and has different ones that you can try," she said.

Because hearing aids can be a major financial investment, Village SHHH members shopped around for them carefully and compared notes often. Yet they were reluctant to advise one another on which aids to buy. "It depends on your hearing loss, what kind you get, what things you need," Sarah said.

"I was happy to see that *Consumer Reports* does not rank hearing aids like they do other products," Dr. Melanie Harris, a speech pathologist, said when she visited us. "And the reason I was happy to see that is, in our clinical experience, a hearing aid that might fit Walt, that Walt might think is a wonderful instrument and just serves his purposes perfectly, might not fit or do the same kind of job for the rest of you. Because everyone's hearing loss is different, everybody's tolerance for amplification is very different. There are many, many kinds of instruments out there, but we find people have very different reactions to those instruments."

Hearing aids differ, but their three main components are standard from aid to aid: a miniaturized microphone, a transmitter, and a receiver. "Every hearing aid works on the same principle," Ann once explained to the group. "There's a tiny microphone that picks up sound, transmits it to an amplifier which increases its loudness, and the receiver sends it into the ear mold." The result is a "gain" in decibels. For example, with her hearing aids, Sarah experienced a gain of 30 to 40 decibels, moving her aided hearing loss from the profound to the moderate-to-severe range.

Until recently, most hearing aids sold in the United States were linear analog aids. "Except for miniaturization, they were basically the same aids for almost thirty years," an area audiologist told chapter members in 1997. "All the major changes in hearing aid technology have come in the last few years." These changes include the manufacture of true digital and digital programmable aids and of directional and omnidirectional microphones (see Ross 1997, 1998).

In January 1998, a retiree named Frank came to the meeting with the November 1992 "hearing aid issue" of *Consumer Reports,* a copy of his audiogram, and some pages of handwritten notes. He had just had his hearing tested. "I've just been diagnosed with a mild hearing loss," he said, "particularly in my left ear, but I've only noticed that in talking with my wife, which I've been told is quite common for some reason." A few of us chuckled.

"Anyway," he went on, "I'm beginning to explore what devices there are, and which are better. . . .There's the digital programmable"—Frank looked down at his notes—"my audiologist mentioned three companies under that; then the truly digital, [he gave a brand name], which they hope to get this month. So if anybody has any information on those things, or on companies which make these things, or experiences of where to go, I guess I'm asking for your help."

"I would follow what your audiologist recommends," Sarah said, "because it depends on your hearing loss. But when I say follow what your audiologist says, don't go totally by that. If you're not happy, or if you feel they're not giving you the opportunity to try things out, then I would try somebody else. And another thing—if you haven't been wearing a hearing aid, it takes time to get used to. Everything's going to seem so much louder."

Ironically, first-time wearers often complain that hearing aids make them hear *too much.* When Dad got his first hearing aid, he complained about the street traffic, the morning birds, even the mantelpiece clock—all seemed to be closing in around him. He had a terrible time in restaurants.

"Hearing aids?" Ann asked once during a group discussion. "They're machines! They do not pick up what *you* want to hear. They don't pick up those vowels, they don't pick up the consonants, they don't pick up the word. They'll pick up everything, just everything around us.

"Some models can be adjusted to the different frequencies, but, again, they're not perfect. They can't pick out speech and amplify that. Even the smallest hearing aid remains on the outside. The person's own defective hearing system must still take that message from the ear to the brain. [And the brain] must decode the imperfect message that it has received. It's like a bad phone line. Making it louder does not make it clearer."

"When you lose your hearing," Tom added, "this ability to exclude what you don't want to hear no longer functions. And that can't be corrected with hearing aids." (See also Bakke 1995: 15.)

Today, some hearing aids come with "zoom" features or directional microphones that enable wearers to focus more on desired sounds in noisy environments. Laura, in her seventies, wore a pair of digital programmable aids that came with a small remote-control device that enabled her to alter reception according to the sound environment. "I usually press the three," she said, when I asked to see it.

"What does that do?" I asked.

"It cuts down on the din," she answered.

"How do you like it?" Miles asked.

"Well," Laura paused a moment, "it's better than nothing." Her answer drew nods and belly laughs.

As Laura found, not even the most sophisticated hearing aids enable people to hear only the sounds they want to hear. Wearers still have to work hard at picking out speech.

"All the hearing aid is, it's an *aid* for your hearing," Sarah explained at the meeting Frank attended. Sally was also there as a newcomer; she had just moved to the area to live with her daughter.

"I know a lot of people have the expectation, the hearing aid will bring my hearing back," Sarah said to Sally and Frank. "They think, 'I won't have any more problems,' but that's not true. It's going to seem like there's a lot of loud noise and everything's going on. But don't give up. Keep going back to whoever you get your hearing aid from, because sometimes they can readjust settings or come up with other suggestions. It takes time to learn how to filter out some of those sounds."

After all the talk about noise, Sally wasn't sure she wanted a hearing aid. She already had a "noise problem." "I'm aware of my hearing loss," Sally explained, "but there's another thing. When I hear a loud sound, it shatters me. I'm shaking like a leaf if a dog barks. I've been around animals all my life, but I've never had that. Loud noise really does disable me. I am truly disabled for a moment until I work it out."

"I think the problem you're having is something audiologists call recruitment," I suggested. I looked for help in Miles's direction.

"I think that's the right term," Miles said. "Recruitment means that something about your ear makes loud sounds even louder. I have it, too. My [new] hearing aids have what they call automatic gain control—the louder a sound is, the more it reduces it. . . . I'm supposed to go back so they can fix it up with the computer. . . . The big point is that they can adjust it so that you can keep from being overloaded with noise and yet have a good response—try to make a compromise."

Miles went on to explain more about hearing aids, then continued with a description of assistive listening devices.

"Is there anything you'd like to ask or add?" Sarah asked Frank and Sally.

"I want to ask Miles something," Sally said, reaching for the microphone. "Are you, or were you, an engineer?"

"Well, I still feel like I'm an engineer," Miles answered.

"Well, all of this is very simple and straightforward to you," Sally sighed, "but, for me, I want to rruunnnn!"

When people lose their hearing, they may think that all they need to do is write a check for a hearing aid. Yet, as members of Village SHHH explained, hearing aids don't "correct" hearing like glasses correct vision. Hearing aids are tools the wearer has to learn to get used to and tools they have to learn how to use.

"Some people just can't get used to them," a member named Martha said. "I—I completely depend on mine. But you just got to keep it in there long enough to put up with it."

"The reason to get one when you're younger and healthy," Miles told Frank, "is that you get used to it."

"Cause when you get used to not hearing," Sarah added, "when you finally get a hearing aid—"

"—it sounds strange," Miles concluded.

Most people who wear hearing aids will still hear sounds unequally. Some sounds will be very loud; others, too soft. And wearers will still have to work at picking out speech. Yet Village SHHH members who used hearing aids couldn't imagine life without them. As Joel summed up, "With my hearing aids in, I can hear Maggie!"

What happens when people don't get the hearing aids they need? A hearing aid dealer who spoke to the chapter suggested that they could lose the capacity to understand speech. "I've had people I've tested probably ten years ago, and they come back in and say, 'Well, I'm ready for a hearing aid, would you run a test on me?' You amplify sounds; all they hear is noise. To understand conversation, they've waited too long."

I asked Ann about this phenomenon. "It's concentration," she answered. "It's keeping up, keeping alive in what you're hearing, and wanting to. If you let that go, then you don't have the energy to hear anymore. Because it does require tremendous energy to concentrate all the time."

While growing up, Ann wore a hearing aid in one ear. "I have found over the years that my speech discrimination has gone up to about 97 percent in my fitted ear," she said. "This other ear I can't do too much with. Had I known years ago that it was going to be like that, I would have gotten hearing aids in both, not just in my better ear."

Experience with parents who never succeeded at using their hearing aids pushed several members to join the group. Asked to introduce herself, one woman said, "I came because I want to avail myself of an education in hearing loss before I get to the point where my mother is. She waited too late and has not benefited from a hearing aid at all."

At chapter meetings, members were glad to see others with hearing aids. Often, a hearing aid indicated a good ear—that is, one that could benefit from amplification. Walt commented, "Frequently the hard-of-hearing person only hears in one ear—usually the one with the hearing aid."

Sometimes hearing loss in one or both ears is so great that a hearing aid can't help. Jan, a retired high school science teacher, was born with no middle ear on the left. She began losing hearing in her right ear as a teenager. "I have been going to audiologists and otolaryngologists for years," she said. "None has ever recommended a hearing aid."

When Sarah was fitted for her first hearing aid at the age of six (a body aid with a cord running from the aid to a bulky receiver), it took her a year to learn to use it. Before that, her parents used a microphone and speakers at home to amplify their voices for her. Sarah got a second hearing aid in high school, after an ear infection damaged her "good" ear.

Now in her fifties, with new hearing aids, Sarah is hearing sounds she has never heard before. "After I got these," Sarah pointed to the high-end analog aids she had been wearing for almost a year, "[My husband,] Terry, would put tapes on and have me try to pick out what instrument was playing. And part of it was having to learn to identify it, but after he helped me identify which was which, I could identify some of the instruments.

"I can hear Terry leave the house in the morning now, which I've never heard before, if I'm listening for it. Of course, it has to be relatively quiet. And I can hear the cat meowing—a soft meow from across the room."

Most SHHH members felt they couldn't stay active in the hearing world without their hearing aids. Yet they all had friends or acquaintances who refused to wear aids or to have their hearing tested.

"I live out at Carolina Trace along with six hundred other people—most of whom are partially deaf," Miles said. "Some of them, most of them, won't admit it."

According to a brochure published by SHHH, Inc. ("Hearing Loss: You Can Do Something about It!"), only one-quarter of Americans who could benefit from hearing aids actually wear them. What are the reasons for this resistance?

Members had some ideas: People don't recognize that they have a hearing problem; a family member "does their hearing for them"; they don't want to spend the money, or have the money to spend. At a state conference, a speaker from the national SHHH organization mentioned that less than 5 percent of the cost of hearing aids is covered by insurance.

But the main barrier, most members believed, is social

stigma. As Ann once angrily put it, "[People think] only old people wear them, or deaf and dumb. Where do newspapers print advertisements for hearing aids? On the obituary page! And they'll say, at the same time, 'Hide it. Most people won't even know you're wearing a hearing aid.'"

While vanity keeps some people from wearing aids, it pushes others to choose particular instruments for appearance's sake. "This creates a dilemma for hearing aid dealers," said Dr. Taborn, a clinical audiologist who visited the chapter. "Should they sell the aids people want, or the aids people need?"

Dr. Taborn related a sales encounter he had recently witnessed: "The whole sales pitch was directed toward size. There was no concern directed to technology, options, how [aids] work in different situations, whether [the aid] was even appropriate to the gentleman's hearing loss. It was purely based on the fact that he needed a hearing aid, and of the four hearing aids that were available, this was the smallest, and that's what he wanted."

Dr. Taborn did not blame the dealer entirely. "The consumer is concerned about high prices," he said, "but he is also concerned about looks, ignoring some of the more basic technological needs."

In choosing hearing aids, SHHH members learned to discount the visual aesthetics. Within the group, most members wore behind-the-ear (BTE) aids. Because they are larger, these aids are usually more powerful than aids designed to be worn in the ear (ITE) or completely in the canal (CIC). Laura said, "My [old] hearing aid dealer didn't want to sell me a behind-the-ear aid. He said most people don't want them. They're too conspicuous. I asked him, 'Which is more conspicuous—wearing a behind-the-ear aid or saying, WHAT? WHAT?'"

Walt also told his audiologist to give him a bigger aid. "I had one of the real tiny ones once, but, for several reasons, it wasn't satisfactory and I took it back and I told him, forget the cosmetics, the vanity. I want to be able to hear better."

Many Village SHHH members also preferred behind-the-ear aids because they are easier to manipulate and can take larger, longer-lasting batteries. Even more important, BTE aids are more likely to come with built-in telecoils and t-switches. These provide two benefits: (1) they enable wearers to take advantage of "hearing aid-compatible telephones," and (2) they enable wearers to use the assistive listening system known as the audio induction loop. (These benefits are discussed in Chapters 4 and 8.)

Lipreading

For hard-of-hearing people, their ears are the problem, but for many of them, their eyes and lips are part of the solution.

"I just wanted to know if there is anyplace you can go to learn how to lipread," a visitor asked at a chapter meeting. "I'm not interested in signing, but I am interested in lipreading." An older man who had just moved to the area said he was interested, too, but had not been able to find a class. Ann suggested the visitors call the speech and hearing clinic at the university hospital. "The official name," Ann commented, "is speechreading."

Hard-of-hearing people rely heavily on bodily and facial cues for communication. Members laughed in recognition when Maggie commented, "Let me get my glasses so I can hear you." They disagreed, however, about the extent to which they could "read" speech. Abe, a retired dentist whose hereditary hearing loss began when he was in his fifties, told me he did not read lips, at least not consciously. But he said he always watched speakers' faces to gauge their feelings and, hence, their intent.

Cora, who also began experiencing hearing problems in middle age, from unknown causes, agreed with Abe. "I don't read lips very well," she said, "but I do look at faces. This makes a lot of difference."

It irked Ed that so many men have beards and mustaches. "It's hard to see their lips," he said, "or tell if they're smiling."

To pick up as many facial cues as possible, at chapter meetings we sat in a circle or around central tables. When large attendance required that we sit in rows, people stood up to talk and waited for others to turn their faces toward them before speaking.

When I interviewed Cora at her home, she asked me to sit in a particular chair. Near the end of our talk, I asked if she had asked me to sit there for a particular reason. "Oh, yes," she said, "this was with the light." The chair faced the window so that natural light fell on my face. Cora told me she needed all the help that she could get—besides her hearing loss, she was also beginning to suffer from vision problems.

Although Cora and Abe didn't think they could read lips, others believed they lipread "naturally."

"I bet you're going to ask me about lipreading," Walt said when I talked to him and his wife. "With me, it's instinctive." Karen, who grew up with hearing loss, also called her lipreading "a talent."

"Where did you learn to lipread?" a visitor asked her.

"Ah, well, Gallaudet [University] told my parents you can't really, you can't teach it," Karen answered. "Certain people are better at it, but you can't teach it. It's a talent, like playing music." Sarah also believed that she was a "natural-born lipreader."

Is lipreading a talent, or a skill that people spend different amounts of time and energy learning? Ironically, calling lipreading a talent may unintentionally discredit the concentration and work it requires.

In her memoir, *The Feel of Silence,* Bonnie Poitras Tucker describes her lifelong struggle to communicate by reading lips. Unable to hear from early childhood or perhaps birth, Tucker raised a family, graduated from college and law school, and now practices law in her own firm. Yet, as Tucker also explains, lipreading has its limits. In her law practice, she needs people to finger-spell or write out their names. In the courtroom, interpreters must mouth "not legal" instead of "illegal" since "legal" and "illegal" look the same on the lips.

"Sometimes, in reading lips," Sarah commented during her interview, "words look the same—for example, *light* and *night.*"

"Speechreading, lipreading—do you think it's easy?" Ann asked one day at a chapter meeting. "It's *not*. You can really only read 30 or 40 percent that's on the lips. The rest is word association."

As a representative to various councils and committees on disability, Ann often attended meetings at which hearing persons expected her to speech-read them. Sometimes she liked to turn the tables.

"I like to do this," she demonstrated to chapter members. "What am I saying?" Ann opened her mouth twice, forming words without sound. "You *know* this person," she teased, when no one answered. "He's on TV all the time." Her lips formed the name again. "Anybody know?"

"No!" she answered. "Nobody can! That is Teddy Kennedy. Very easy. I mean, nobody can get that one. And then, when President Bush was around, saying, 'Read my lips: No new taxes'—they couldn't even read that!"

"I've been to speechreading classes," Delores told me in her interview. "As for speechreading, there is nothing more difficult to do. It requires intense concentration, and it requires good eyesight, and it requires good imagination because you're seeing one or two things on the lips, and the other three or four things are not seen. They are at the back of the mouth, they're consonants or something, and by the time your mind has seen those two things, your mind is saying, 'Okay, what's that?' You're onto something; *they're* onto something else."

After one meeting, I complimented Karen on her speechreading. I was surprised when Karen replied, "But sometimes, I'll *fool* you. I'll say, 'Yeah, yeah, yeah.' I think I, you know, catch all of it, but I don't. My parents have trouble with me on that. . . . I misread people a lot, misunderstand a lot." Karen, in her late thirties at the time, lived in an apartment attached to her parents' house. Until she got a teletypewriter—discussed in Chapter 8—she relied on her parents to answer the phone.

Jan used speechreading almost entirely. All her life, she'd relied on seeing more than hearing. "If I don't *see* the other, and if they don't speak with moving lips as well as teeth and tongue, I have great difficulty," she said. "It's exhausting!"

To understand a speaker, Jan told me in her interview, she had to focus her attention completely. When she had houseguests, she got up to cook before her guests arose, and straightened up after they retired at night. "I can't do anything when I have company," she said, "because I have to be able to pay attention. I have to get up two hours before anybody else does and stay up for an hour or two after everyone else has gone to bed, and I am literally exhausted, and it is largely the exhaustion of trying to attend to someone else."

Even *with* hearing aids, hard-of-hearing people can't initiate and carry on conversations as easily as those with normal hearing. To have a say, people with hearing loss have to attend closely to the visual as well as the verbal cues in the setting. As Sarah put it, "If I'm focused on what somebody is saying, the sound helps, but . . . it's only part of the whole thing. In other words, I've got to see how the lips are moving to put it together.

"You know," Sarah confided, "when Terry and I were first dating, he told some of his friends he wasn't going to chew gum. He thought I might think he was saying something!"

Eyes and Ears

Many people fear losing their sight. Hard-of-hearing people view the loss of hearing as the more disabling. "You know," Sarah said, "Helen Keller said if she had a choice between being blind or deaf, she would prefer to be blind, because hearing is communication—it's social. It profoundly impacts all the relationships."

When my son was born, one of the first things I did was check to see if his ears looked right. I took my mother-in-law's advice to lay my newborn down carefully in his crib, making sure his ears stayed flat against his head. She and I viewed ears as important primarily in an aesthetic sense. They shouldn't be too big or stick out too far.

When Adam was five, I took up drawing as a pastime. On vacation in a cabin for a week, I decided to work through the book *Drawing on the Right Side of the Brain* (Edwards 1989). When I got to the section on drawing faces, I was astounded. For all those years of grade school, I'd drawn the eyes high up on the face and the ears along with them. In fact, I learned from the book, and then from looking, eyes and ears sit halfway down our heads. Both are *central*.

To the person who is hard of hearing, ears can never be aesthetic objects. These sensory organs are what connect us to a larger world of interaction and meaning.

Hard-of-hearing people hear bits and pieces of conversation, parts of words, some people's voices but not others. Many live in a world of confusion. Some opt out, withdrawing from social interaction. Others use hearing aids and lip-reading as bridges—as connectors to the hearing world.

4 Assistive Listening Devices

Since passage of the Americans with Disabilities Act (ADA), "more and more public facilities are bringing in assistive listening devices," audiologist Jill Jackson told Village SHHH members at a meeting in the fall of 1997. "Normally, you'll see a sign that says 'Assistive Listening Devices Available.' They will always, 100 percent of the time, work better than just your hearing aids."

Hearing aids help connect speaker and listener, but not at a party or across a large room. When hard-of-hearing people are in these kinds of settings, they need the help of an assistive listening device.

"With an assistive listening device (ALD), you have a direct link," Jill Jackson explained. "When someone is on stage talking, their voice has to travel all the way to you to be picked up by the microphone on the hearing aid. That's a long way for it to go when the ideal listening distance for anyone wearing a hearing aid is less than six feet. With an assistive listening device, it goes directly from the speaker into your ear."

Using "the Loop" at Chapter Meetings

At Village SHHH meetings, we used an assistive listening system known as the audio induction loop. Before each meeting, Miles or Tom would roll out a loop of wire around the

41

seating area. When plugged into an audio power amplifier, the loop created an electromagnetic energy field (Compton 1989: 12). By sitting inside or near the loop, anyone whose hearing aids were equipped with telecoils could receive the microphoned sound directly through their hearing aids.

As Village SHHH members gathered for our meetings, those who had telecoils in their hearing aids reached up to turn them on. Flipping the t-switch from the M (microphone) to the T (telecoil) setting turned their hearing aids into audio induction receivers. As Delores explained, "With the loop, the sound is still coming across the room, but I'm not hearing it across the room. I hear it *right here.*" She grinned and pointed to her ears.

"I guess everybody knows, or recognizes, that this is an audio loop around you," Miles said as we passed the microphone around one day for introductions. "And if your hearing aid has a tele-switch, a t-switch, you should try it. It transmits . . ."

"Do you turn the hearing aid off?" Lennie interrupted.

"In the hearing aid, there may be a switch, between the on and the off," Miles said. Another member went over to Lennie to help.

"It's not a whole lot louder than the regular thing," Miles was saying, "but it eliminates noise; it's a lot clearer."

"Oh," Lennie exclaimed. "It is!" Although he had never used them, it turned out his aids had telecoils.

Besides using their t-switches to hear at chapter meetings, members used them on hearing aid–compatible telephones at home or work. As Jill Jackson explained, "Many telephones have electromagnetic leakage to them. The telecoil in the hearing aid is compatible with that."

One day Tom was rolling out the wire that made the audio loop and taping it to the floor with gray electrical tape when he stopped to ask Ann, "You use your t-switch, what, thirty times a day probably?"

"Oh, yeah," Ann answered.

"At least," Tom countered.

Ann began an informal poll of the members. "Do you use your t-switch?" Ann turned to Sarah.

"All the time," Sarah answered quickly.

Ann continued around the room until she got to Walt. "Walt, you don't have a t-switch on your aid?" she asked.

"It doesn't work," Walt answered.

"Walt—Walt has two," Tom said, and smiled.

"But it doesn't work on either one," Walt countered.

"Ah," Tom said. "It's an interesting problem. Magnetic field is related to size . . . in other words, the size of the hearing aid. So, the bigger the coil in your hearing aid, the stronger it is."

At the time, I didn't understand Tom's point. Was he suggesting that Walt's hearing aids were too small? At any rate, Walt seemed to take Tom's remarks as criticism.

"Well, it used to work," Walt said, apologetically. "I used to use it on the telephone."

I learned later that some members often needed to boost the power in their hearing aids to use their telecoils effectively. This sometimes meant choosing more powerful behind-the-ear hearing aids.

On the Internet e-mail list, subscribers referred to the value of telecoils again and again. In one posting, a man lamented having purchased hearing aids without either telecoils or a method for adding them. At the time he purchased his aids, he didn't know about telecoils or realize their importance. In response to his posting, another subscriber only half-jokingly suggested he "sue the manufacturer": "Any hearing aid manufacturer who fails to include a coil, or provision for one to be added, should be, in succession, deafened, emasculated, hung, drawn, and quartered, and then have his license removed forever. And that's just for starters!"

"Wow!" the original correspondent replied. "I hadn't felt that strongly about it. I do, however, feel that way about one previous audiologist."

This exchange prompted another account. "I had t-coils right from the beginning," the subscriber wrote. "Only problem was, the audiologist never explained to me what they are and how to use them! I had to find out from other HOHs [hard-of-hearing people]. Now when I talk to audiologists, I stress the importance of explaining/teaching about t-coils and other assistive devices."

In a chapter meeting, Maggie reported a similar experience. "We took Joel to the audiologist two weeks ago and found out that Joel's hearing aids were practically dead! We've ordered new ones, but I had to *ask* for a t-switch. They didn't suggest it. I said, 'It's *got* to have a t-switch.'"

The longer people belonged to Village SHHH, the more expert and particular about technology they became. Most long-term members knew the difference between audio loops and other assistive listening systems and could speak knowledgeably about teletypewriters, closed-captioning, and alerts for phones, doors, and fire alarms. Newer members asked them for advice and, sometimes, for demonstrations. Yet most seasoned members agreed that behind-the-ear hearing aids with t-switches were *the* best tool for making use of residual hearing. As Tom once said, "There's all sorts of other hearing devices—there are interpreters, there's

FM systems, there's infrared, there's computer-assisted note taking—there are different kinds of ways, but the principal way is a behind-the-ear aid with a t-switch."

Today, many SHHH members also choose behind-the-ear hearing aids because they come with a combination microphone/telecoil option. "If you're looking at buying a new hearing aid," Jill Jackson told members, "you're not going to find good telecoils in in-the-ear aids. You're definitely not going to find good microphone-telecoil (MT) switches in in-the-ears. That's really a behind-the-ear thing—and if I were going to make an investment in hearing aids at this point, I would definitely make it with something that had both an option of a telecoil and a microphone-telecoil switch built into it. Cause when you go to T, you shut everything else off. I tell a lot of my patients that wear binaural hearing aids that if they go to the theater, use the t-switch on the ear that's away from your friend or spouse and go to MT in the other aid so you can still hear what they say to you."

Trying Out FM

Village SHHH members liked using the loop at monthly meetings, but FM and infrared systems were far more common at theaters, public auditoriums, and church. With an infrared system, sound is broadcast as invisible light waves; to receive them, the user has to check out a receiver and sit within sight of the system's transmitter. FM systems broadcast sound as radio waves. A receiver set to the programmed frequency can pick up the radio signals anywhere within the facility and, sometimes, outside it.

On a winter day in 1992, Village SHHH members had a chance to try out an FM system at the art museum on the local university campus. The museum had just purchased the system and invited chapter members to see how it worked. As we hung up our coats and gathered around the reception desk, a docent pointed to the small microphone clipped to her shirt and to the transmitter she wore. She handed out earphone headsets and small box receivers, about the size of a pack of cigarettes.

Ed quickly removed his hearing aids, put on the headset, slipped the receiver into his pocket, and hurried off to the men's room. Maggie helped Joel on with his headset, then asked for one for herself. "Maybe I can write about it," she said in my direction. Although she was not hard of hearing, Maggie had already written one article about hearing loss for the local newspaper and done a radio interview on the topic. I followed her lead. As I was adjusting the pads around my ears, Ed returned from the washroom. "This is amazing," he announced to the docent. "All the way to the men's room and back, I could hear you! I could hear the whole thing!"

Eight of us shuffled off behind a smiling docent—Joel and Maggie; Ed and his wife, Mary; Tom; Ann; Laura; and me.

At the first painting, the docent's voice drew me in. The FM system delivered her words directly into my ear, creating an intimacy that I found almost shocking. At the same time, I found I was communicating with the others with smiles and head nods. I could see how effective an FM system like this would be in a classroom setting, linking student to teacher. But I also wondered about its effect on interaction in the larger group. I noticed that Ann wore her headphones at an angle, keeping one hearing aid on and that ear out. "I just like to have one ear in and one ear out, you know," she said. Ann was using the headphones in a way that hearing aids reproduce today with the MT setting.

Ann had extensive practice with FM systems. The assistive listening equipment business she and Tom owned had installed the museum's system. At the end of the tour, Tom took a moment to explain why it was needed.

"A hard-of-hearing person very seldom can hear any farther than five or six feet," he said. "If you go back farther, already there's been too much attenuation of the *sh*s, the *th*s, the *c*s, and like that. Sound doesn't travel."

The docent nodded. "With this mike," she said, "we're talking at six inches."

"That's exactly right," Tom said. "The hearing aid is really only designed for short distances. If I get over here"— he stepped back a few feet—"you can't understand what I'm saying."

Tom's remarks pepper my field notes. Yet, in thinking about the tour, my strongest memory is not of Tom or Maggie but Joel.

Able to hear with the FM device, Joel blossomed. A retired surgeon who served in the medical corps during World War II, Joel carries a slowness of aging exacerbated by early Alzheimer's disease, extra pounds, and arthritic knees. Yet several times during the tour, he commented insightfully on the artwork, identifying one sculpture as a Hebrew letter and naming a piece of military equipment on another. Even his step seemed lighter. Connected so closely to the voice of the speaker, Joel could make the most of his surroundings and the occasion.

Personal Technologies

The art museum trip in 1992 was the first time many Village SHHH members used an assistive listening system other than the audio loop. Since then, members have had many more opportunities to use assistive systems. Many use assistive listening devices regularly at movie theaters and church.

As a retired minister, Ed likes to hear every word of his minister's Sunday sermon. He was therefore disappointed when his church's FM system gave him poor results. When he told his audiologist that the ear buds his church provided were not working very effectively, Dr. Martz suggested he take along an audio neck loop. That way, Ed could still wear his hearing aids.

Neck loops are personal versions of the audio loop we used for our chapter meetings. The loop goes around the neck like a lariat, then plugs into a small box receiver. Users then access the amplified sound through the telecoils in their hearing aids, adjusted for their particular hearing loss.

"Our church had some FM devices, and the button is supposed to go in your ear," Ed said. "Well, it works, sort of. A week ago Dr. Martz gave me this loop to try. Now I get the FM box from the church, put this loop on, and set my hearing aid to t-switch. I can hear everything. I can even hear when the minister whispers to somebody next to him."

Snickers of laughter erupted around the circle.

"So," Ed said, ignoring the laughter, "if any of you have access to FM technology and you have a hearing aid with a telecoil, why, talk to somebody about getting a neck loop."

As in Ed's case, when people's hearing loss is profound or severe, they need to combine the ALD with their hearing aid to get the most benefit. Meg, an activist from a neighboring chapter, explained. "The earphones will just raise the level of the sound, but oftentimes our hearing doesn't have a flat curve on the audiogram. We need all the sound to go through our hearing aids, because they are adjusted so those high sounds are raised and lower-frequency sounds are not."

"But what should we tell a theater owner?" a chapter member asked. Meg had been encouraging us to ask for ALDs whenever we went to a play or a concert, or to see a movie.

"We should explain that headphones are good for the mild, maybe the moderate, loss," she answered. "But we need to educate them that they don't work for everyone. We need a variety of devices to meet the needs of the mild, moderate, and severely impaired person."

At his church, Miles received FM signals through his hearing aids by using a silhouette adapter. "It does the same thing that the loop does except you don't have the loop around your neck, you just have this [small adapter]," Miles said. "It hangs over your ear and it sits down alongside the hearing aid. You have a cable, of course, running from the box [receiver], but it works the same way [as the loop]. [The adapter's] magnetically coupling into the hearing aid."

Another way people can connect receivers to their hearing aids is through the direct-audio-input (DAI) feature available on some behind-the-ear hearing aids. The DAI is actually a socket into which the user plugs a "boot." A wire from the boot can then be connected to the receiver.

Miles also carried his own receiver. "I've got one of those little boxes that's tunable," he said. "If I get tired of listening to the preacher, I can tune over to the Methodist church— it's only across the street."

"You did that?" Karen squealed.

"I did that," Miles answered, grinning. "I did that accidentally. There's a couple other things on that frequency channel, too, not churches. I don't know what they are; I didn't take the time to find out."

"Our church has FM, too," Laura said. "It works very well as long as the man doesn't forget to put it on the charger."

"If the minister forgets to turn on his microphone, which he did once," Ed commented, "I don't hear anything."

"What you have to do is point to your ear and wave at him," Miles said, demonstrating with large strokes.

Assistive listening systems work to bring sound from a microphoned speaker into a listener's ear. In settings where there are no microphones and several speakers, hard-of-hearing people may need their own individual ALD.

One option is to purchase hearing aids with direct audio input, which can be used with a cord and a hand-held directional mike. By pointing the microphone, the signal-to-noise ratio is improved. That way, users can zoom in on whomever they want to hear.

Another option for people who have their own FM receivers is to put a conference microphone in the middle of a discussion table. Although Sarah sometimes did that, she preferred setting up her own audio loop. The loop she had came with a kit that also had modules for FM and infrared.

Today, at least one manufacturer has come out with a personal FM system (with tiny microchips) that boots directly into its company's behind-the-ear hearing aids. This obviates the need for a separate box receiver. There is also a new wireless microphone on the market.

Five years after we visited the art museum, I returned to see if there had been any changes.

"Do you wear a hearing aid?" the attendant said when I asked to see the assistive listening equipment. She brought out a utility box with several small receivers. In addition to earphones, I noticed a neck-loop option.

"Oh, that's great," I said. "You offer choices. Do many people use the equipment?"

The attendant leafed through a three-ring notebook. "All three receivers were checked out for the opening of this new exhibit."

I remembered Jill Jackson's instruction to chapter members. "Whether it's a headset, ear bud, or a neck loop for the hearing aid, just go ahead and wear it. You'll catch the sermon, and you'll catch the jokes."

5 In Public

Members of Village SHHH were having an informal gripe session when Sarah looked around the table and asked, "Have any of you missed hearing your name being called at the doctor's office?"

Walt quickly raised his hand. "I think my experience is only significant because it happened at a hospital that was full of doctors who handle hearing.

"On a Friday morning, I went uptown to the bank, chatted with everybody, and, before I got back to my office, which was two blocks, I'd lost my hearing in my other ear. I went to see my doctor, and he gave me an emergency slip to the [ear, nose, and throat clinic], and so I got over there right after lunch, and at five o'clock they were getting ready to close and they came and said, 'What are you here for?' and I showed them my referral, and they said, 'Well, we looked for you, why didn't you answer?' and I said, 'That's why I'm here—I can't hear!'"

A few members chuckled; others shook their heads. We moved on to other topics, but Walt's story stuck with me. What was it that kept Walt sitting there quiet all afternoon? I needed some help in understanding the psychology of hearing loss to learn the answer.

A few weeks later, I opened the mailbox to find an announcement. Tom and Ann had relocated their assistive listening equipment business and welcomed visitors. I called the number and made an appointment.

Stigma, Energy, and Voice

Ann and Tom's shop sat just off the highway at the outskirts of a neighboring city. Ann met me at the door with a welcoming grin. Although it was early April, she had already started her tennis tan. Only the reading glasses on a cord suggested middle age. I set down my tape recorder so we could greet with a hug.

"Hey," Tom's voice rumbled in from a back room. As he moved toward me to shake hands, I was struck by the gentleness within his large frame. Next to Ann's trim neatness, Tom looked like a scientist just out of the lab.

We slid into swivel chairs around the conference table in their main showroom.

"I'm stuck," I began. "I'm supposed to be writing a chapter about being out in public, but I've come up against some kind of wall I don't understand."

I told her about Walt's experience in the waiting room. "I can understand how Walt could sit there and not say, 'When are you going to see me?' but I don't know how to explain what goes on to allow that to happen."

"You wouldn't let that happen, would you?" Ann said gently. "If you had been there twenty minutes, thirty minutes, you would go up [to the desk]."

"I'm pretty patient," I laughed. "I would probably sit there an hour."

"Right," Ann prodded, "but then you'd eventually have gone up there."

Ann paused, then continued more softly. "It's a stigma that hurts. And it really does hurt. It's something that you don't want to be, you don't want to admit. He would not want to admit that he didn't hear his name being called.

Plus, he is a very nice person, he is patient, and he would hate that it happened.

"Now, of course, we think the staff should be more aware. After all, it *is* an ENT clinic! They should be going around to see why he didn't show up. But we should take the initiative straight off and say, even if this is an ENT clinic, 'I can't hear you, please come and get me.'"

I thought of Walt. Now enjoying retirement, he had been a university financial officer at the time of the clinic incident. "At that time, there was nothing [to help me]," he once told the group. "Oh, people expressed sympathy and all that, but I had to scramble to do things like find out how to rig the phone to make it work." Used to overseeing major accounts and a large staff, Walt became a person others found hard to talk to. Always in command before, he had lost more than hearing; he had also lost voice.

"I remember when my father died," Ann said, bringing me back to the present. She explained how, after a night without sleep, she ended up at an airport waiting for the connecting flight that would eventually take her to New Zealand.

"The plane wasn't due to go for, oh, another five hours," Ann said, "so I went up to the staff there and said, 'Look, I'm really tired. I'm probably going to sit here and just close my eyes. Please wake me if something happens. I will not hear your announcement.' And they didn't."

"They didn't?"

"They didn't do it. And then, I did kind of wake up, and they had moved that plane's departure to around the corner, and when I woke up I thought, 'Oh, my God, I've missed the plane!' No one came and got me. So there, it didn't work. But I did go and tell them, I need some help.

"So that means you're continually fighting," Ann added.

"You're fighting people for your, our, just for basic help. We can't do it ourselves. But it's very tough—because this is not just this day, this is tomorrow, and it's tonight. It's continual, and it never stops.

"It's something that . . . you have to have this extra energy to be assertive every day. And I do find that sometimes I don't have it. But I know tomorrow I'll be all right. I'm just tired. I have to acknowledge that I don't feel like hearing today, and I don't feel like fighting everybody, so I'm just going to shut up and be quiet."

Before joining Village SHHH, I was unaware of how much hearing loss causes exhaustion and loss of voice. Or of how much dealing with it depends on dredging up energy, and speaking out.

"I remember you once said that small changes in the environment can make a big difference," I reminded Ann. "Things others don't notice, like an air conditioner."

"Yes. That means that when I go into a place, I have to be, first of all, very aware of the environment. I have to arrive thirty minutes early to survey the listening environment—well, that's what I do, because I have to hear, you know. Is the air conditioning on? Is the fan going? Where's the sunlight coming in?

"Then, I'll choose my chair, where I think I will hear best, but often that's not the one I'll end up with because the speaker may wander up and down, or I can't see the overheads, or see well enough to speech-read. And often, the sound system's not working; then I try to solve the problem.

"So that all these things, if you want to be in the world, you have to take care of. A lot of people aren't willing. They just want to get up and go like you do.

"I can't go like you can, and just show up and hear.

Maybe I have batteries in my hearing aids that aren't fresh. That has to be right. I have to be not tired. If I'm tired, I'm not going to hear very well.

"So, it is a lot of understanding of yourself, but that's taken years. For me to say that now, it's all very easy, like I've known that for years, but I haven't. It's really been quite . . . it's been a learning experience."

We sat in silence. Suddenly it hit me: I had chosen the wrong chair. With all my research on hearing loss, I sat where Ann had to stare into the glare from the window to read my lips.

"Am I sitting in a bad place?"

"No, I'm okay," Ann answered softly.

"I, I just realized that I . . . I write these things down, and then . . ."

"Well, that would be up to me to say, because I know that you're receptive to my saying."

Ann shifted slightly in her chair. "I don't know how you would bring this into this chapter that you're writing," she said slowly, "but my mother's here. And it's been, ah—I owe everything I am today to my mother, okay, because she really did a lot. But I still say, she didn't understand. Nobody helped her understand my hearing loss. She was by herself, and she and I loved each other very much, and she gave me all the support that she could, but she didn't understand what I was facing outside. In my own little home, I was very protected. But I had to get out and work, and this is where, oh, gosh—this is going round and round—I'm remembering a lot." Ann sank deeper into her chair. When she spoke again, it was about her nephew.

"My nephew is deaf," Ann said carefully. "He's twenty-four now. But when they discovered he was deaf, around ten months old, when he was not responding to sounds, then between the two families, my family and my sister-in-law's family, it was, whose side did this come from? The other side was blaming my side. My mother said, no, it's not her side. Like, I didn't have a problem—it's not our side.

"Well, all these years, I've tried to say, 'Mum, it doesn't matter whose side of the family it's on, it really doesn't matter.' But that's where the shame comes in, the stigma. That's how bad it was. It was not my side of the family that this comes from.

"Now, nobody signed for my nephew. My brother did not sign, but I'm saying again, I had a wonderful family. So I've got two things going—I came from a beautiful family, but the shame was there."

"So, there was a contradiction—love and acceptance and support of you, but also an uneasiness?"

"It was uneasy."

"You had a problem, and they didn't want to . . ."

"They didn't want to face it." Ann's voice was almost a whisper.

Tom's voice came from across the table. "It was only— and you correct me if I'm wrong on this," he looked at Ann, "it was only two years ago, maybe four, that Ann's mother, in one of her visits here, they got into a big argument, and Ann says, 'I'm deaf, I'm deaf.' And her mother didn't—'Oh, no, you're not!'"

Ann shook her head slowly, remembering.

"See, what we consider hard of hearing is, basically, deaf," Tom said. "It's a degree of deafness. Almost all people who are deaf have *some* hearing."

"To me," Ann said, "I've come to the conclusion, if I can't understand what the person is saying, then I might as well be deaf. Because I'm missing this word or that word, and I'm guessing to put it together, and I may make a fool of myself if I guess wrong. I have not been able to hear every word of the sentence. So, to me, it's easier for me to say I'm deaf. And I'm quite, I'm very happy with that, but that took me many years.

"Getting back to my mother, I think I was fortunate, because I did have support and love. Most people don't have the support I had.

"Talking about older people, why would Walt wait for hours? He missed his name being called, so he waited there for hours and hours. How do you explain that? This is a hard-of-hearing kind of loss. We've lost—we lose a lot, the confidence, because we're not sure, did we hear or not? He's hurt. He's hurt. That's where you have to get over that hurt."

"Well," Tom shook his head, "that's partly true. People are people though. I mean we always tell the story of one lady who hadn't been out of her house in seventeen years. There's a zillion different situations hard-of-hearing people can fall into. My father is the best example. He was in a wheelchair right before he died, basically deaf. He was a professor, right? But the last five years of his life he preferred to roll himself into the corner because he didn't know how to get himself going again."

"We did try to help him," Ann said, "but he and your mother wouldn't let us. Your mother would say, 'I can't stand the noise of the TV,' so he would turn it off. And we were saying, 'Here, let us help you.' Uh-uh. His wife was too important, so he didn't hear. So, this is, it's—I think it's damaging, it can be very damaging, unless you catch it."

At a meeting in 1992, Betty passed out a handout on communication tips. The "first rule' for hard-of-hearing people read: "Communication is a two-way street. The hard of hearing person must make as much effort as the hearing person."

As Ann made clear, this rule is an understatement. To make a go of being out in public, hard-of-hearing people can't merely make an equal effort; it often must be greater.

Going places means going early and being prepared. Then comes the task of getting others in the setting to also take pains. Not all hard-of-hearing people have the energy. Not even Ann can find enough energy for every encounter. Outside the circle of words and activity so much of the time, hard-of-hearing people often find it easier to stay quiet. The exhaustion and stigma of hearing loss can bring about a complicit silence.

I remembered something Ann had said at a chapter meeting. We had just finished doing a role play of a restaurant setting, deciphering the server's scrambled phrases to give them some sense. "Lap shower" became clam chowder; "make tomatoes with fish eyes," baked potato or French fries.

"It's a little farfetched," Joel had complained at the end of the skit.

I secretly agreed, but Ann stood up to defend how realistic it was.

"Oh, I don't know," she said. "I've always been left behind when the waitress says the dressings. Blue cheese, and then she goes on. I always get the same thing. As for the special of the day, I've never had the special of the day!"

Here was Ann, the group's star activist, admitting that she also occasionally stayed quiet.

Public Access

Near the end of the interview, Ann told me about a recent occasion when she had exercised voice.

"I was appointed to [a disability commission]," she said,

"and I thought, 'Well, geez, I'm going to have a hard time there, even though many of them are in wheelchairs, and they're talking about every other disability'—and I did. I had a hard time, and I had to stop them all, stop the meeting, because they can all *talk*. You know, everything goes on like this, and suddenly here comes this woman who can walk in . . .'"

Tom wheezed with laughter. "She can *walk*," he said, "but she can't *talk*!"

"Yeah—the wheelchairs are rolling around, and, ohhh! I can't hear! Ohhh."

Ann, a tennis player in a room full of people in wheelchairs, turned out to be the one who most needed help.

"See," Tom said, insistent, "when a hard-of-hearing person is in a meeting, the meeting has to change. People perceive a meeting to be give and take—yelling, standing, jumping, whatever. That's a, that's an American custom as a good meeting."

"Spontaneous," Ann added.

"That won't work with deaf and hard-of-hearing people." Tom softened his words with a smile. "And I don't think it's a good old thing. Even last night," he said, referring to a public meeting he and Ann had attended, "we had one lawyer that I had to stop; he jumped up fifteen times to say something. And I said, 'You're not saying anything until you put the microphone on.' Fifteen times, I had to."

Ann intervened to finish the story. "And the lawyer said, 'Well, why do I have to do this?' And Tom told him, 'Because these people *need to hear*!'"

I thought about our chapter meetings, where passing the microphone around paced the give and take; where we sat in a circle to face each other; where members like Ann stood up to speak; where we took the time to make sure that everyone was included.

"Participate," Tom concluded. "That's really the key word. Because that's the word that makes you equal. If you can participate, you do have access. Anybody can listen. You can go to a movie and listen. Listening is one thing, participating is—not many hard-of-hearing people participate."

Everyone with a disability faces problems participating in public settings. For some disabilities, the barriers are obvious—narrow doorways, tiny print, high curbs. For other disabilities, the barriers are subtle, even invisible. Hard-of-hearing people move about freely in public places. Yet they do so within a shroud of garbled words that has the potential to disconnect them from everyone present.

Ann was not content to give up her voice when she went out in public. As hard as she sometimes found it, she made the effort to arrive prepared and to speak out. Yet even Ann sometimes felt she needed a break.

I hope that the Americans with Disabilities Act of 1990 will make participation easier for people like Walt and Ann. In my vision of the future, assistive listening systems, note takers, and interpreters will be as commonplace as wheelchair ramps. Yet this will happen only if people with hearing loss tell others what they need and ask for help. In this educational mission, people who speak up can make all the difference.

6 Dos and Don'ts

About fifty of us watched as Dr. Samuel Trychin pulled the loop over his head and secured a mike to his shirt. Clad in jeans, his graying hair pulled back in a ponytail that revealed a behind-the-ear hearing aid, Dr. Trychin was holding a special open session on communication strategies during a two-day workshop for area mental health professionals. A retired professor of psychology at Gallaudet University, Dr. Trychin continues to conduct workshops nationwide. He also writes a column for *Hearing Loss,* the SHHH journal.

"What do you want to talk about? What questions do you have?" Dr. Trychin's friendly glance put us all at ease. A real-time captioner typed his words into a computer; they appeared on a large TV screen placed near the front of the room. Between the TV screen and Dr. Trychin, a sign language interpreter held a questioning pose.

A small woman with curly white hair raised her hand. "I want to know how I can get my hearing back," she said.

"You want to ask me . . . how to get your hearing back?" Dr. Trychin repeated the question.

"Yes," she nodded.

"Pray," Dr. Trychin laughed, and a ripple of laughter passed through the room.

"And it won't help," he added. A few of us laughed again.

"If you're lucky enough to have a conductive hearing loss, you can get it back," Dr. Trychin said, more seriously. "But if you have a sensorineural loss—which is probably 90 percent of us—it has to get worse and then you can get a cochlear implant and then you can get it back."

Within our local chapter, only Sarah had expressed interest in getting a cochlear implant. The procedure involves implanting electrodes in the inner ear near the auditory nerve (Gantz 1992). A small speech processor, worn outside the body, changes acoustic information into electrical signals that the brain then interprets as sound. Although cochlear implants do not restore normal hearing, many people who have them can, with training, eventually hear well enough to use the phone. Cochlear implants are still new and expensive ($35,000 to $40,000 for the surgery and first-year training and follow-up [Roeser 1994]). And, because the surgery entails risks of complications, implants are currently approved only for a fraction of the hard-of-hearing population.

A middle-aged woman raised her hand. "I would assume that the first problem people have with loss of hearing is depression. How can you avoid it?"

"How can you avoid depression that goes with hearing loss?" Dr. Trychin repeated. "Well, I think it's not hearing loss itself that produces the depression but the communication problems that go with hearing loss, right? For most people, it's the lack of connection with other people that produces the depression, . . . and that can improve. There are all kinds of things we can do to understand better what people are saying."

Hearing aids and assistive technologies are one way to maintain or regain the human connection. Changing our behavior is another, and, by far, the harder.

Tips for Coping with Hearing Loss

Get Rid of Negative Thinking

The middle-aged woman raised her hand again. "You tell people you are hard of hearing and that they need to talk slowly, and they forget in fifteen seconds. That's very easily interpreted as a put-down."

"That's right!" Dr. Trychin exclaimed. "That's why we have to be careful how we think! We can get off on all kinds of fantasy trips about how, if she really loved me, she'd remember to talk slowly all the time. That's nonsense. What people are doing is what human beings do: They forget. They only remember to do what you ask them to do until they get interested in what they're saying again.

"Nobody out there, nobody, has been trained how to communicate with somebody who's hard of hearing. No one. But yet we expect them to all know. And we expect that once we tell them, they'll remember forever. . . . You can live with someone for thirty years who has a hearing loss and still talk to them from the next room, right? I mean, that's like wasting your breath. And why do we do that? We do that because we are HBs—human beings!"

Diagnose the Problem and Provide Feedback

Alice, a woman who sometimes attended our Village SHHH meetings in her role as regional coordinator, raised her hand. "I find that I myself frequently forget; when I'm with other hard-of-hearing people, I forget the rules of the game. I turn my back. I start talking too fast. One of the members of our chapter pulls me aside over and over—'Alice, you're talking too fast.'"

"See," Dr. Trychin said, "she says that she has a hearing

loss and she does the same thing. . . . Hard-of-hearing people come up and say, 'Alice, you're talking too fast.'"

Dr. Trychin turned to address Alice. "You have talked fast your whole life, right?"

"Yes," Alice answered.

"Nobody thinks about how they talk," Dr. Trychin said. "That's an unconscious level. To change it, you have to bring it to the conscious level. The only way you can do that is with feedback. Like the woman we had in one group, I was talking too fast for her, so she takes a Ping-Pong paddle and she tapes paper on both sides. One side she writes, 'Please slow down.' The other side she writes, 'Thank you.' The whole week, she waved it back and forth."

Dr. Trychin imitated the woman.

"She controlled my rate of speech," Dr. Trychin explained to a laughing crowd. "It was wonderful! It took the responsibility off of me. I can't remember, when I have a group of people in front of me, it's hard to remember to slow . . . down . . . more . . . for her. So—she did it."

To do something about a problem, people need to know more than its name. They need to know its hows and whens and whys.

"It took me quite a long time to realize how much more specific I needed to be," a woman named Laurel wrote in to the Beyond-Hearing Internet e-mail list. "I'd get frustrated by how people would overgeneralize when I said I was hard of hearing. Now I see how this label is really not all that informative. For example, if I just say, 'Could you repeat that,' people are left to their own devices to figure out what the problem is. If I don't tell them I'm deaf in my right ear, they don't know they need to get my attention first if they're on my right side."

Another subscriber agreed. "I try to explain why part of

the sentence was missed, such as, 'We are standing too close to the dishwasher' or 'The light was bad on your face and I missed some nonverbal cues—let's move over here.'"

"Just realize that this will go on forever," a third subscriber responded. "You will constantly be educating, they will always forget, and you will always need to remind them. Lovingly, of course."

"Remind them, remind them, remind them," Dr. Trychin said back at the gathering. "But not verbally. If I interrupt Howard every fifteen seconds to say, 'Please slow down,' fifteen seconds later, 'Please slow down,' fifteen seconds later, 'Please slow down,' he's not going to stay with me very long. He's going to find some excuse to be out of there.

"So what we have to do then is, I have to say, 'Howard, because of my hearing loss, I need you to talk slower than you usually talk. But I know that you're going to forget to do that. I know that. So, is it okay with you that, if you begin to speed up again, I tap my ear to remind you to slow down? Is that all right?' Okay, now we have an agreement. So he slows down and fifteen seconds later, he speeds up. I tap my ear. Or, I could make a little sign and put it in front of me, and when he speeds up, I just point to the sign.

"It's not rocket science, right? But these are the kinds of things that we can do to help ourselves stay on the planet earth and in communication with other people. . . . What I'm talking about are the small nuances of communication that make all the difference between whether people will comply with what we need or not."

To change behavior, people need to be told what behavior to change. How they are told can make all the difference.

"We're always telling people that we have a problem," Dr. Trychin continued. "That says nothing about a solution.

We have to stop saying 'Huh? What? Excuse me, could you repeat that,' and start staying things like, 'Because of my hearing loss, I need you to look at me when I talk.' 'Because of my hearing loss, I need you to slow down a little bit.' 'Because of my hearing loss, I need you to raise your voice, and I'll tell you when it's right.'"

Dr. Trychin searched the faces around him. "Do you see the difference?" A few people nodded their heads. "Now I'm giving you a solution to a problem, not just telling you I have a problem. . . . It's not your problem, it's really mine, so I need to say, 'Because of my hearing loss, I need you to . . .' Then it becomes my problem and you are much more likely to be helpful and not feel criticized."

Hearing loss presents a contradiction. Although hard-of-hearing people may often feel unheard, it takes voice to make the hidden known.

Some hard-of-hearing activists have begun wearing brightly colored hearing aids to advertise and normalize their invisible condition. Yet these can also escape others' attention. "Did you know I have super-glued several large rhinestones onto both my BTEs [behind-the-ear aids]," one mailing list subscriber wrote, then added—"but they still don't get noticed all that much, and I wear my hair short and off my ears—go figure!"

The problem is that even people who know about someone's hearing loss still need guidance on how to help. Unlike some other disabilities, hearing loss provides no ready clues about its nature, extent, or accommodation. Consequently, hard-of-hearing people must be their own best friends—cueing others into their need for a hearing, letting others know when and why they haven't heard.

Don't Bluff

"Here's a nice one," Dr. Trychin said. "Don't bluff. Now I know that hard-of-hearing people as a group don't do this."

His statement was greeted with raucous laughter.

"But we don't want any more of this"—Dr. Trychin tilted his head and maintained a frozen smile.

"We all have our bluffing look, right? So why even bother? We're not getting away with it anyway. It's a terrible, terrible thing to do to yourself, because it kills your self-esteem. It murders your self-esteem, because bluffing by definition means to pretend you're understanding when you don't, and you know you're doing it and it's a cop-out. The long-term effect is deadening."

Alice raised her hand. "Bluffing is very insulting to the person you're talking to because it means that what you're saying is not all that important to me, so I can afford to miss it."

"That's right," Dr. Trychin said. "If I find out ten minutes later that you don't have a clue what I've been talking about, it's not going to make me as a speaker very happy. The first thing I'm going to think about is that you don't give a damn about what I'm saying. So it's going to produce relationship problems. It's deadly for us, so we really want to stop doing it, because it's not practicing effective communication— which is when I don't understand you—to make a quick diagnosis of why I don't understand you and offer a solution. . . . Oops, because of my hearing loss, I need you to slow down. Oops, because of my hearing loss, I need you to take your hand away from your mouth when you talk. Because of my hearing loss, we need to get away from this machine when we talk."

"But hearing people bluff, too," a woman in the audience objected. "I mean, they don't always pay attention. Bluffing is sort of a way of communication. If it's not something really important, if it's just a general story . . ."

"She said hearing people bluff anyway," Dr. Trychin repeated the woman's statement.

"So you pick your situations," the woman went on. "I mean, if you're just in a pleasant conversation and it's not something super-important, you don't really always have to go, 'Wait a minute.'"

"She's saying that there are going to be situations in which it's not so important to understand what somebody's saying," Dr. Trychin repeated, then turned the statement into a question. "It's not so important for them that you understand what they're saying? Why are they talking?" Nervous laughter rippled across the room.

"There's general conversation, and . . . " the woman began, then trailed off.

"Hearing people make a lot of the mistakes that we make," Dr. Trychin said. "But also last week three guys jumped off the San Francisco Bridge. Does that mean we got to do that? . . . It's not always apparent what's important to know and what's not important to know. And my concern with bluffing is that it becomes habitual. If somebody does it once in a while, I don't care. But if people do that as a matter of course, they lose their jobs, they miss important information, they lose relationships."

If it's not done right, telling others when words have been missed can get on their nerves. But, by not telling them, the hard-of-hearing person gives the false impression of having heard, or of passing as hearing. This makes hearing loss into something negative to be hidden or overcome. And it pushes the pretender further out onto the margins of the hearing world.

Halfway through my interview with her, Jan asked if she could relate an "anecdote." We were sitting across from each other at her kitchen table with my tape recorder running.

Jan was now retired, but she had worked for years as a high school science teacher. She never told anyone at work that she was hard of hearing. Although she got along well in the classroom setting, other situations were not as pleasant.

"Since I was new [at the school]," Jan said, referring to a point midway through her career, "I was honored to sit at the headmistress's table. There were eight of us, and I was madly trying to follow the conversation when I realized that almost everyone was finished and I had not yet begun eating lunch. I either had to be talking or watching, it was that kind of a situation.

"So, in a rush, I popped the whole of a biscuit in my mouth. I looked up to see if anyone had caught me at it, and every eye at the table was on me. It was clear that someone at the table had asked me a question; I didn't know who. After an interminable time, when the saliva completely evaporated, I had a mouthful of biscuit crumbs. The headmistress said very slowly, as one does to a mentally deficient child, 'Where do you live?' So I masticated a while, everyone watching, and finally spat out my address."

In this example, Jan's worst fear was realized. Because the others at the table didn't know about her hearing loss, she was left in the spotlight for someone to rescue. Although she was brought back into the group, it was at something less than adult status.

Develop Realistic Expectations

John was frustrated when he posted a note to the e-mail list. He wondered whether it was sometimes better to stay home than to bluff his way through uncomfortable situations.

"Well, it happened again last night," John wrote. "I went out to dinner with four friends only to find that, as usual, I came home totally in knots of frustration over not being able to understand the conversation at a table of four of us. Up until last evening, I never showed my frustration to people and just kept smiling, but last night I showed some anger with myself and it was noticed by my friends. . . .

"What I want to know from all of you on the list is this: Would I be making a correct choice in telling my family and friends that this type of situation is so hard on me that I prefer not to dine out and am more comfortable in a get-together in a home situation?"

"It is a sign of emotional health when people stop putting themselves into no-win situations," Terri posted back to John and the other list subscribers. "Unless you have a workable solution to the problem, for example, an assistive listening device or sign language, it would seem to me that a one-on-one situation would be much better for you and your family."

"In some situations," Carla agreed, "I find it is amazingly helpful to simply stop expecting to hear and understand. When I do not ask myself to do the impossible, I find my frustration is eliminated. . . . In a restaurant, I focus on enjoying the food, the atmosphere, and the mood of the group. However, I do not seek out these situations. My friends are proving most responsive to my needs. For example, social lunches are now regularly scheduled in my office with take-out food to allow us a chance to enjoy some good food and yet still enjoy talking."

"You have to have some realistic expectations of what you can expect to understand," Dr. Trychin said near the end of his talk. "[Some] social situations—you're there to soak up the good vibes, the ambiance, the good feelings, or whatever. . . . We have a woman—she has a severe bilateral hearing loss—who went to a Thanksgiving dinner with fifteen or sixteen people, and she came back and reported, 'I had a wonderful time. I focused on my food, I focused on the textures and colors of people's clothes, and I just soaked up the good feelings of the whole family around the table. I didn't try to understand anybody. It was wonderful. People I wanted to talk to, I made appointments. I'll see you around two o'clock and we'll catch up on how things have been. How about four o'clock, can we go for a walk and talk?'"

Most hard-of-hearing people want to stay connected to the hearing world. But many members of Village SHHH and of the e-mail list agree that sometimes it's better to set boundaries and let go: Exit one situation and create another.

Carla, the subscriber who said she sometimes found it helpful "to simply stop expecting to hear and understand," went on to explain. "I find that by not always expecting myself to understand a situation well enough to participate in it, I am free to make decisions about accepting invitations and also to make decisions about how I want to meet my needs. I have basically told my friends that if they would like to share an experience like a dinner out with a group with me, I am delighted. If they would like to have a conversation with me, great! Sometimes these two goals are mutually exclusive. Other times we can make accommodations and adjustments that accomplish both goals. This is simply the way it is. Wishing it was otherwise will not make it so."

"Realizing this was a real breakthrough for me," another subscriber, Lynn Piper, agreed. "It allowed me to relax and 'pick my spots' as to where I wished to direct my energy and efforts. . . . I try to engineer one-on-one situations as necessary, even having gone so far as to suggest we have our drinks in the parking lot on at least one occasion. Accepting that there are simply things I cannot do has been the key for me. Once I got past this, I was able to begin to learn to enjoy what I CAN do, and even get a bit of a kick out of the strategy planning."

Hard of hearing since her fifties, Laura had recently had a stroke that left her with even worse hearing. Still, she knew that if she were going to get anything out of an informal gathering, she would have to be the one to take control. "If I want to talk to somebody," Laura said in her interview, "I'll try to push them into a corner if I can. We were at a party the other night. There were about twenty-five people, but they, ah, they just sat around in the kitchen. Everybody was there except me and a friend. We went out on the porch."

To deny or not deal with hearing loss obviously can have negative consequences. Bluffing or staying quiet can leave people feeling isolated. Yet hard-of-hearing people don't have to stay at the margins of the hearing world. Groups like SHHH enable hard-of-hearing people to be with others who share their difficulty and understand. Out in public, or within the family, people can also use the strategies Dr. Trychin recommended. By telling others when and why they haven't heard—and the conditions under which they can hear better—hard-of-hearing people can reconnect to others and rejoin the group.

7 The Environment

"I'm sitting down watching TV," Sarah is telling the group, "and I decide I'm going to let my dog out and I open the door, and, ohhh! I didn't know it was raining."

"At our house, we don't have any protruding eaves," Laura said, "so I have to close the windows when it looks like rain. But sometimes I forget, and, of course, this is partly because I just forget, but it's also because I can't hear that it's raining in."

The world is full of sounds and sound cues. Hard-of-hearing people live in this world but may miss out on some of the sounds that others use to monitor their surroundings. Discussion turned to this loss of environmental sounds during a panel at a state conference.

Ted and Dee had organized the panel, which featured four married couples. Dee had a severe hearing loss, and Ted's, in the mild-to-moderate range, was "getting worse." "I've always had acute hearing," Ted commented, "so going from being able to hear a pin drop to not being able to hear some particular noise from the night is a considerable change."

The panel included a Deaf couple, a hard-of-hearing couple, and two "mixed" couples. For example, Mary identified herself as culturally Deaf; she used sign language as her means of communication. Mary's, husband, Bob, had lost his hearing at age nineteen. Although he also signed, he used a hearing aid and identified himself as hard of hearing and oral.

74

Audio and Visual Cues

As Mary began, an interpreter voiced her signed words. "Well, I really feel that we don't have a problem [in our relationship]," Mary said, "because we make jokes about our misunderstandings. But one problem that we've both had to adjust to is, when he goes upstairs and I'm watching TV downstairs, you know, it's like, I need to know where he's going because I can't hear anything, so I can't hear whether he's walking, or where he's going. You know, did he go outside? To take out the garbage?"

"I grew up as a hearing person," Bob explained, "and this just isn't a hearing thing. I mean, you don't say, 'I'm going into the kitchen, I'm now turning on the . . . ' You don't think about it, but those are audio cues. . . . It's a courtesy within the Deaf community, and a lot of hard-of-hearing people need it, too, they really do. But I still forget at times to tell Mary what I'm doing."

Nancy and Roy understood Bob's point. "As a Deaf couple," Roy signed, "we base our decisions and reactions on what we see, not from what we hear. When we got our children—both of them are hearing—we had to adjust our perspectives on life both on what we see and what our children hear, or what my wife thinks she hears.

"One example, every time we leave the house we're always saying, 'Is the water on? Is the bathroom okay? Is everything off?' We always imagine the water running because we don't hear the water running. Once we were watering the lawn outside and we left it going all night; we didn't hear it. We woke up and went outside, and it was soaking!"

"Not to mention our water bill skyrocketed," Nancy signed vigorously. "That's one of our most often fears, and it's happened to us several times. It happened one time in the middle of the night. I went to the bathroom and somehow, luckily, I happened to hear the water running—I was close enough to be able to hear it run because everything was so quiet I was able to hear the noise. And I checked and, sure enough, the water had been running for about four hours. And then another time, I was washing clothes and had them in the tub and it broke and the water ran all over the floor, and I had no idea that happened.

"Oftentimes I feel that I hear something," Nancy continued, now signing more slowly, "and then I realize, no, there wasn't anything there. And then I wonder if maybe my kids were upstairs screaming, that might have been what I heard, and then I tell myself, no, no, I don't think so—so occasionally things like that happen."

"One example that might be familiar to hearing people," Roy signed, "is dealing with a real noise or sound. We deal with a visual noise. For example, last Saturday we were rearranging the family room so that our children running in and out of the kitchen wouldn't go through our field of view. So, our children, really, they adjust well to our deafness, and we try to adjust to their hearing as well."

"I want to add that the children also need to let us know where they're going," Nancy signed. "Like, if they go to the restroom or they're taking a shower or they're using the telephone or going to a friend's house, sometimes they don't let us know, but that is something we ask them to tell us. It's a must. So they've become accustomed to that. It's natural to them because they were raised that way."

From Sound to Silence

After Nancy and Roy sat down, Ted and Dee stood up. "The thought occurred to me," Ted said to Dee, "that even though you're classified as severe hearing loss and I have a moderate hearing loss, we're still dependent on oral cues and communication."

"Yes," Dee said. "I was impressed with Nancy and Roy saying they don't hear, period. They know they don't hear, that's the end of it. That's not how it is for me. I hear some of the time. I'm fine some of the time. And then my [hearing aid] battery dies, or I take the thing off, and I'm essentially deaf. I can't hear the water running; I don't hear the clock going. And it's a very sudden shift sometimes. It's very difficult."

For most hard-of-hearing people, taking off their hearing aids marks a shift in worlds—from the more familiar world of hearing to a far quieter one. They lose sounds they may have come to depend on at other times.

When Sarah brought her new daughter home from the hospital, she could hear her crying during the day but not when she took her hearing aids off at night. After the first few nights, she decided to leave her hearing aids in when she went to bed.

"That seemed to work okay," Sarah told the group, "but, in the back of my head, I knew I really wasn't supposed to be doing that. So, well, after a few days, I developed sores in my ears, and the doctor said, 'What's the matter? Your husband can't listen for the baby?'"

Sarah's daughters are now grown. Today's parents have more options. A transmitter and receiver, placed next to a crib, can pick up a baby's cries and send them to other rooms in the house. Visual alerts are also available for doorbells, telephones, and smoke alarms. People can receive signals through a flashing lamp, a strobe light, or a vibrating pager. And people can purchase a visual alert system for the car that warns them of approaching sirens.

When Sarah travels for her work, she tries to write or call

ahead so the hotel will be ready with visual alerts. "Some places only furnish specifically what you request, like a flashing fire alarm or an amplifier for the telephone," Sarah told Village SHHH members, "but one place I stayed at had a little suitcase, and they gave it to you to take to your room, and it had everything in there, and you could pick out what you wanted in your room."

To monitor and negotiate the physical environment, people who don't hear well must rely more on their eyes and on visual cues. Yet some environmental sounds have no clear visual substitute. For example, hard-of-hearing people may not be aware of people who are nearby but outside their field of vision.

"This has happened to me quite often at work—opening the door," Sarah said one day at a chapter meeting. "We have a flight of steps to go up and down with doors off of every level. So, anyway, oftentimes I get ready to open the door, and I don't hear a person on the other side walking up to the door, and then we both try to open the door at the same time, or the door flies open and I run into them."

A woman in my writing group shared an incident involving her husband, Jim. "He doesn't hear people coming up behind him," Camille explained, "so sometimes he steps on people. Once one of our daughters fixed him some hot coffee, and she was bringing it to him. Jim was excited, talking about a movie or something, and he didn't hear Molly, and he threw his arms out and his hand caught the cup and the boiling coffee spilled and scalded her chest. We ended up at the emergency room. And it was such a shame, because we'd all been in a good mood, and she was doing something nice for him."

Feedback

In an ironic twist, hard-of-hearing people sometimes inadvertently make environmental sounds that they themselves can't hear. Roy laughed, "Often, when we're out eating or at home, our son will say, 'Dad, you're making a lot of noise. Could you keep some of that smacking down to a minimum?' So I adjust my eating habits for him."

Few hard-of-hearing people can hear the high-pitched squeals their hearing aids emit if the ear mold is improperly seated, the volume too high, or an object too close. "You're whistling," Mom would tell Dad several times a day, and he would reach up to reposition his hearing aid, watching her to see if he had eliminated the feedback.

"My hearing aid sometimes gives feedback," Karen said to the group, "and I can't hear it, even though I know it hurts. When I was in high school, the first day of class the teacher came in and she went to answer the phone and there was nobody there. So the people in the back of the class raised their hands and they said, 'That's Karen's hearing aid ringing, not the telephone.' . . .

"Another time I was in line at the bank and I saw people looking around like they were hearing something they couldn't identify, and I just started doing the same thing, like I didn't know what was happening."

"The only time I hear it squeal," Sarah said to Karen, "is, like if I'm hugging somebody, or getting up close, I can hear it go *bee-bombbb*. Years ago when *The Bionic Woman* was playing on television, my husband said, 'You're the only woman I know that gives a bionic response.'"

To get around safely in the world, people in the Deaf community learn to depend on visual cues. People who use hearing aids hear environmental sounds some or much of the time, but then a battery goes dead, or they take off their aids, and the sounds they normally rely on are gone. To negotiate their environment comfortably and safely requires hard-of-hearing people to make perceptual and interpersonal shifts: to ask others to show where they are or tell where they are going; to purchase and install visual or vibrotactile alerts; and even to invite feedback on the sounds they, too, contribute to our audio environment.

8 Telephones and Television

Walt was reading the newspaper on his balcony when he saw an acquaintance on the sidewalk below. "Hello," he called down.

"I immediately regretted it," he told me in his interview. "I started missing about 90 percent of what he said."

"What did you do?"

"Started looking for a graceful way to get the thing terminated. 'Gotta go,' I said. 'Wife's calling,' I said."

Talk has a geography, a spatial dimension. We use words to cross the distance between us (Gurevitch 1989). From the balcony, Walt opened a space for conversation. Unable to hear his acquaintance and too far away to read his lips, Walt closed the space and turned away.

Telephones

Telephones extend the reach of conversation from a few feet to around the globe. At the same time, they disembody the conversational arena. Unable to see the person at the other end of the line, hard-of-hearing people continually relive Walt's balcony experience.

In the middle of a discussion of telephones, Tom stopped and shook his head. "Hard-of-hearing people have the worst time with the telephone. It's not well understood. People go to all kinds of extremes to solve the telephone problem."

The "telephone problem" became apparent one day when Ron temporarily filled in as chair for Sarah.

"Ron is chair today," Maggie told the assembly.

"Yes," Ron said. "Somebody called me on the telephone and asked me to help with this." He looked around the room until he noticed Jan. "Was it you who called me?" he asked.

"No," Jan answered, "I think it was Sarah."

"People are so familiar with their names, they mumble," Ed suggested. "For instance, I pick up the telephone. 'Ed?' 'Yes.' 'This is mmmmpphhhmkk. I want to tell you about the meeting next week.' I finally have to say, 'Now, who did you say this was? Would you spell it?' Then I feel stupid when they spell, M, A, R, Y."

Because hard-of-hearing people have difficulty hearing when they don't have any visual cues, many simply avoid the phone. "I avoid the phone like the plague," Sarah told me in one of our conversations.

"I just stopped using the phone," a visitor to one of the meetings announced while discussing her problems at work. "They put amplifiers on my phone, which is not really very good. Now I just tune them out. 'Oh, I didn't hear the phone ringing.' 'You answer it.'"

Hard-of-hearing people rely on face-to-face interactions, not the phone, to cement relationships. Yet, since phoning remains a background expectation in our culture, even friends and partners who understand how difficult phoning is for hard-of-hearing people can feel slighted or neglected.

"Hard-of-hearing people don't use phones the same way," Sarah's husband remarked at the end of one meeting. "Some of the normal communication patterns that people engage in, like, 'Hey, I'm going to be half an hour late,' don't happen."

Hard-of-hearing people avoid phones but rarely abandon

them. They need them for physical safety. Sarah recalled an incident from her years at home as a young mother. "I spotted a fire," she told the group. "I called the fire department and said I can't hear, but there's fire in my closet. I gave the address and the phone number and I repeated it several times to make sure they got it because I didn't know, I couldn't hear anything, and then I hung up. . . ."

When Sarah finished her story, Ann asked for the mike. She looked at Sarah, and then from one member to another around the group. "Don't hang up," she said, her voice urgent. "Never hang up. Leave the phone off so they can trace the call."

For many people, the main way to gain phone access is to use an amplified phone. My father traded in his original phone for one with a volume-control handset soon after getting his first hearing aid. He found that the acoustic feedback from the dual receivers (the telephone's and his hearing aid's) overwhelmed his ability to hear. With the volume-control phone, he removed his aid and turned up the volume.

Within the group, Ron, Ed, and Laura had volume-control phones. Other members had tried using volume-control phones and didn't like them. "The volume control will increase volume 30 percent," one member commented, "but you will have background noise, and that gives me a worse problem." She used a hearing aid with a t-switch and a telecoil.

"This is Joel's hearing aid," Maggie demonstrated on a day we had several visitors. "And this, this little toothpick thing," she leaned across the table to point it out, "is his t-switch. When he talks on the telephone, he just turns that tiny switch."

"Does my hearing aid have a t-switch?" a visitor asked.

"I don't know," Maggie answered. "You'll have to look."

With the t-switch flipped to the "on" position, hearing aids receive sound directly as electromagnetic waves. "In the handset [of the phone] is a coil, an electromagnetic coil," one member explained. "The coils in our hearing aids are compatible with that."

Yet not all phones are "hearing aid compatible"; nor do "compatible" phones work with every aid.

"Ah, the telephone," Ann sighed during her interview. "All the telephones are different, the hearing aids are different, you have to match them. That means you have to buy telephone after telephone, until, suddenly, you've got the right connection."

People also have to learn how to use their t-switch and hearing aid with the phone. "One thing to keep in mind, if you are using a hearing aid with a telecoil and a telephone," audiologist Jill Jackson said when she visited the chapter, "is, you can't hold the phone against your ear. If you're picking up the phone and going to T, . . . you have to hold it closest to where the microphone is so that you're picking up the electromagnetic leakage through the hearing aid. Or, if you leave [the switch] in the microphone position, you have to [experiment with where to hold] the receiver." Jill illustrated with a cupping motion.

Most long-term members of SHHH regarded telecoils and t-switches as their chief defenses against phone deafness. Yet for some whose hearing loss was severe, even t-switches didn't help enough. Some hard-of-hearing people turn to teletypewriters (TTYs), otherwise known as text telephones (TTs) or telecommunications devices for the deaf (TDDs), and Relay Services.

Members of the Deaf community have used TTYs to communicate with each other for several decades. With these devices, they simply type their messages back and forth through telephone lines. Since the 1980s, however, the availability of Relay Services has made telecommunications possible when only one of the parties has a TTY or text telephone. Specially trained operators, through whom the call is placed, transcribe spoken responses into type.

"With the TTY," Ann told me in her interview, "I've got backup. If I can't hear you on my t-switch, then I have the option, I can ask you, since I have a TTY, would you call me through Relay."

When Relay Services began in North Carolina, the company's account manager drove three hours on a Saturday morning to talk to our chapter. Speaking through an interpreter, he said that he saw Relay Services as opening up a whole new world of communication. "The idea that you can talk to a doctor, to a lawyer, to your mother—I can't tell you how we lived without Relay," he commented. "Every day at work, I used to depend on my hearing friends to speak for me, and I felt kind of isolated. Now I can do everything that hearing people can do, except hear. . . . It's easy to become independent with Relay Service."

About a year after the spokesman's visit, Karen announced a milestone: She had used Relay to order a pizza. We clapped to celebrate. Then Peggy raised her hand. "When you call," she said, "somebody in [Relay headquarters] will answer, but it goes through all right. It's for people who can hardly hear at all, but you can get a message through real good."

Ann couldn't ignore Peggy's statement. "I guess I'd like to say that if you are hard of hearing but you think you're not deaf enough to use this system, then you must think again. If you want to communicate with your friends, with your grandchildren, but you just hear bits and pieces, that's not good enough. This is the way to do it. This is the way to go. Accept your hearing loss, just accept it, and get on with it. This is the way to communicate. It's the biggest breakthrough in phoning in our lifetime."

Although Ann and Karen loved their TTYs, they noted that using Relay sometimes has its drawbacks. Phone calls take longer, because they have to go through an operator who transcribes the speech, which then appears on the TTY user's visual display. (As a courtesy, most phone companies discount long-distance calls for hard-of-hearing or deaf people with TTYs.) The conversation can also feel unequal when only one of the parties uses a TTY with the system known as voice carryover (VCO). "You know," Ann explained during her interview, "you're saying something to me, then you say GA [go ahead], you're finished, and it's typed to me, and I read it, then I talk back to you, you hear me—but it's not natural. It bothers me because it's not a natural conversation."

"Is it something about the pacing?" I asked.

"The pacing bothers me," Ann answered.

Karen used her TTY often to type back and forth to hard-of-hearing and Deaf friends. "I love it, I love it," she said about Relay. Yet she felt reluctant to use Relay with hearing friends. "I don't want to call Yvonne over at the hospital and tell her, call the Relay number, or call me back on the Relay number. That takes too much time. I tried that with a friend in another office. She said it took too long, and she just didn't have the time."

None of the new technologies makes phone access easy or equal for people with hearing loss. Relay takes time to use and time to get used to. Yet along with amplified phones and hearing aids with telecoils, teletypewriters give hard-of-hearing people another chance to stay on the line.

Television

Television served different functions in members' lives. Some watched little, others, a lot. Yet all agreed: Words on the screen made watching easier. In televisions equipped with electronic devices called decoders (this includes all larger TV sets sold in the United States today), closed captioning appears as subtitled text at the top or bottom of the television screen. Programs that have been captioned are identified by the symbol "CC" in viewers' guides and in the opening credits of each show.

"I like closed caption very well," Frank remarked one day when we passed the mike around the table. "I couldn't use television at all until I had closed caption."

"The most frustrating thing I found," Joel said, "is when I'm listening to TV and it is *not* captioned. I can hear a voice, but I cannot distinguish what they're saying."

Joel's wife, Maggie, had come to depend on the captioning, too. "With it," she said, "I don't have to listen quite as hard."

"That's the biggest point, I think, isn't it," Ann nodded.

"You're not worn out," Walt said.

"Not worn out," Ann added, "and it's just relaxing, like television should be. It's a relaxation, and I can go to sleep like anybody else can!"

Although most members liked television captioning, some said they found it hard going at first. "If you're reading and it's coming fast," Frank said, "you don't have time to see the expression on people's faces. All you're doing is reading to catch up."

"You have to either look at the words or you gotta look at the picture," Abe complained.

"Ann uses the captioning as a backup," Tom explained. "She hears part, but if she doesn't know what she's heard, or is mixed up a little bit, she glances down. You get sort of a habit, and you don't have to watch it all the time."

Over time, captioning has gotten better and faster. Yet members were amused by occasional mistakes. "Did you get the one last week?" Ann asked. "They were talking about the Supreme Court. It was about abortion rights. But instead of putting the Supreme Court, they put the Sperm Court!"

Some critics view television as mindless, passive entertainment. Yet being cut off from television can make people feel out of touch. Thus, when Ed had trouble understanding a news show, he wrote to the television station. "We usually listen to the *McNeill-Lehrer News Hour* at night," he told me during his interview. "And sometimes when they're having some foreign dignitary, they'll run the captions. I find that very, very helpful. I wrote to Jim Lehrer, said, I have two suggestions. When they have political analysts on, please ask them to slow down. Also, when they have someone speaking in a foreign language, and the interpreter, please turn the voice of the original speaker down."

"Did you get an answer?" I asked.

"I got a one-sentence reply from Jim Lehrer," Ed smiled. "Dr. Leahey: 'I HEAR you!'"

9 Music to My Ears

"Maybe some of you heard the Christmas music," Maggie said as she called the meeting to order one Wednesday in early December. As we had been gathering, seasonal favorites played in the background in bass violin and deep piano tones.

"Maybe you aren't able to hear music as a rule," Maggie continued, holding up an album cover. "But this is special music for hard-of-hearing people. It's for people with a limited hearing range. The music is between 110 and 440 Hz."

After the meeting, Maggie played the record again. By then, most people were busy with the refreshments at the other end of the room.

Two weeks later, in an interview at her home, Karen admitted that she had never really enjoyed music. "One sounds just about the same as the other," she said about the hymns her family sang at church. "It's hard to appreciate, let's put it that way." Yet Karen had always been curious about the musical sounds that others heard. "When I was growing up, I always asked my girlfriend, 'What do those sounds sound like? What does that music sound like?' I'd get her to listen in on my hearing aid," Karen laughed, "and she'd say, 'Well, that sounds the same except for a little bit louder than we hear.'

"Later, in high school, I had a girlfriend that did a lot of singing to me. What I mean by that is, she didn't actually sing, she would mouth the words on the radio to me in the car. I'd ride along and she'd mouth the songs for me. . . .

"The other day I was looking at all the Christmas specials on the television, and the closed captioning really helped. I've gotten more enjoyment out of that now because it shows the words, and now I know some of the words of the songs."

"I'm not sure I can understand the words as well as before," Miles said about music and hearing loss. "But that's difficult to evaluate since I can't switch from 'after' to 'before,'" he added. "I seem to be able to participate satisfactorily in my church choir and barbershop chorus, [but] I usually take my hearing aid out when I sing. With it in I hear my own voice too loud and thus have difficulty tuning to the pitches of my neighbors."

Within Village SHHH, Walt and Julie experienced the loss of music hardest. "I've never mentioned this before, and I've never read anything about it," Walt said one day during an open discussion, "but the thing I miss the most is music. By not hearing certain frequencies, I absolutely cannot recognize a melody. The only song I recognize is the *Star Spangled Banner*. People stand up."

Others laughed, but Julie shook her head. "Music is also the biggest loss for me," she said. "I have to ask people, 'What are they singing?' and if I don't hear the lyrics clearly, they'll tell me *Happy Birthday to You*. That's a slight exaggeration, perhaps, but for someone who used to be very involved in music, it's extremely painful for me, not only not to recognize what I am hearing but not to be able to sing." Unable to find a hearing aid that helped with her low-frequency hearing loss, Julie went from serving as her church's soloist to dropping out of the church choir.

On the Beyond-Hearing e-mail list, several subscribers spoke poignantly of a similar dynamic. "When I was a teenager and very hard of hearing," one subscriber wrote, "I used to love singing in our church choir. As my hearing got worse, I compensated by singing louder. I also sang off key. I thought I was doing just fine until our choir director hinted that maybe it was time for me to quit. I had a nice soprano voice and the rest of the choir was following me instead of the organ—which meant that everyone was off key."

"I also was involved in music for a long time before going deaf," another woman responded. "Not singing with a group, but duets and singles as well as piano and organ. I am very lost without my music. Even though I have a CI [cochlear implant] and can communicate beautifully, music is still garbage to me." She advised that people who love music try an assistive listening device. "I would check out an FM system first," she counseled a man who was thinking about dropping out of his church choir. "See if that will help you—with the external mike worn on your collar or where you button your shirt. You may find that you will be able to hear what is going on around you better."

Other subscribers found another way to cope. They shifted musical genres. One man chose piano music in lower ranges and slower tempos, for example, Beethoven's *Moonlight Sonata,* and "some Andre Previn arrangements in a similar range." Another gained a new appreciation for the Vivaldi Bassoon Concertos; a third discovered saxophone jazz.

Sarah, like Karen, avoided music. I was surprised, then, when she mentioned having played the piano and sung in her high school choir. "I was very self-conscious and sang quietly," Sarah explained. "But I can tell high and low [pitch], and they had me [sing in the choir] so I could learn to put some inflection in my voice and not just speak in a monotone."

Of all the people in Village SHHH, Sarah had the voice I

liked most. She spoke slowly and carefully in a rich contralto, with a rise for questions or when she was excited or tired.

Tinnitus

Ironically, many hard-of-hearing people who miss the lyrics or the fullness of music hear their own internal brand of "music" instead. What they hear is a ringing in the ears called tinnitus.

"Do you want to know the program topic that drew the largest attendance across the state?" Alice asked when she visited us as SHHH state coordinator in 1997. "It was a program on tinnitus."

"What's tinnitus?" Laura asked.

"Well, the other name for it is ringing in the ears," Alice answered. "Do any of you have it?"

Of the nine people at the meeting, Miles, Pat, and I raised our hands.

Tinnitus affects one in five Americans. Although many people with the condition have normal hearing, it is more common among people with hearing loss.

According to a brochure published by the Better Hearing Institute (Barr 1996), tinnitus can be caused by outer, middle, or inner ear problems. Wax in the outer ear or fluid in the middle ear can produce temporary episodes. So can taking drugs containing aspirin. In the inner ear, the causes include exposure to noise; whiplash; concussion; tumors; thyroid dysfunction; low or high blood pressure; hearing loss associated with advancing age; and Ménière's disease — a disorder characterized by "pressure increases in the inner ear fluid," dizziness, and distorted hearing.

Yet, in a preface to a textbook on tinnitus, Drs. Jack Vernon and Aage Moller (1995: xiii) conclude that tinnitus remains a "medical enigma." Researchers "know very little about why and how the auditory system, under certain circumstances, can produce a sensation that is similar to that of a sound while no external sound is present."

As I write this, my own tinnitus is a faint treble line. Occasionally, I also hear a rapid chirping I call "my crickets." I loved it when "tinnitus symphony" appeared as a subject heading on the Beyond-Hearing e-mail list. I had been wondering what kinds of sounds other people heard. One subscriber wrote that his tinnitus began as "a 'spring peepers' kind of noise (the cacophony of noise at night in the spring by a swamp)" but progressed to a "constant warbling." Another described his tinnitus as "a cross between a dial tone and a buzz saw, and unchangeable." A third heard roaring and gushing water, and occasionally "a thousand firecrackers going off." "Have to laugh to myself sometimes to keep from thinking they are the real things," he wrote. "I know they are not, because I am deaf. The popping sound is back right now, more like a Morse code. Wish I could decode it. Is someone trying to tell me something?" In closing he added, "Just being able to share this is helping."

In a study of the 1,033 tinnitus patients listed in the Oregon Tinnitus Data Registry she established, Dr. Mary Meikle (1995) found an inverse relationship between the degree of hearing loss and the pitch of the tinnitus: People who hear lower pitches usually have more severe levels of hearing loss.

What do people do about the inner noises they hear? My own case is not so severe that I can't ignore it by getting involved in something else. I hear it most when the house is quiet and I'm lying down for bed. Other people find that hearing aids help by providing a mask. One person wrote that when her tinnitis gets very bad—so bad she thinks it will drive her crazy—she goes to sleep with her hearing aids in. Some people mask the noises with other sounds—for example, a loud clock, radio static, a cassette tape of environmental sounds, or a special "tinnitus masker," worn like a hearing aid.

Clinical experience suggests that people who have "no negative beliefs associated with tinnitus" are less likely to attend to it or to experience it as bad (Hazell 1995: 66). In this vein, several subscribers to Beyond-Hearing said they dealt with their tinnitus by using humor or transforming the ringing into songs. "I was able to focus on [the tinnitus] and get it to play a melody," one person wrote. "For the past week and a half I've been hearing 'Abide with Me.' Since I also hum along at times, my wife told me to 'Change the record,' which I've found I can do. Try it," he concluded. "When life gives you lemons, make lemonade."

"If you could tell me how to tune in Vivaldi," a man responded, "I promise I won't ever complain again."

"It may not really be possible to think tinnitus into tunes or make it go away," another subscriber commented. "But having 'imaginary' music in our heads helps to mask it out. Calypso is great for this because of the beat. Now my husband has been trying to remember the banana boat song because he has had 'Day Oh, Daaay Oh' running through his head. What are the rest of the words? I forget the tunes of songs that I heard before I lost my hearing. Seeing the words written out brings them back."

Although some people are grateful that their hearing aids mask their tinnitus, Neil had an unusual hearing loss that enabled him to hear his hearing aid's constant hiss. "So in quiet times, when I am by myself," he wrote, "I take my hearing aids off and listen to my tinnitus instead." He closed his post with the symbol G, which means "grin."

10 At Home

When someone in the household is hard of hearing, the family struggles daily with communication. As a retired professor of communications, Maggie knew a lot about sound and broadcasting, but that didn't help at home with Joel.

At one of the first SHHH chapter meetings, Maggie described one of the incidents that brought her and Joel to the group. "I ask Joel to pass the peas," she said. "He answered, 'What's that about kidney fleas?'"

Other interactions weren't as funny. Maggie sometimes found herself raising her voice until she was shouting. "With Joel," she said, "I find I sometimes have to shout. And to me shouting means hostile, anger, and yet he doesn't hear me if I shout, and I'm not sure what emotion I'm expressing."

Another family member agreed. "When we repeat ourselves," she said, "we have a hard time keeping our voices pleasant."

"We don't have to be told *that*," a hard-of-hearing member responded. "We know!"

In some families, tension surrounding hearing loss shows up in family members who talk past the hard-of-hearing person, or walk away.

"I hate it when I'm talking and Tom walks away," Ann said. "He walks into another room and he knows I can't hear," she said. "Why does he keep doing that? For twenty-seven years—our anniversary was yesterday—twenty-seven years, and he still walks away."

"Well, I think that one of the things that bothers me,"

Steve said, "is—let's say we're sitting in front of the television, three of us—my wife and I and our son. When that's over, my wife would like to communicate to somebody about it, but she will always turn automatically to my son first, and I figured out the reason is, it's an effort for somebody to communicate with me sometimes and determine whether or not did I catch the whole thing enough so that I could really understand her questions. I wouldn't mind if it would be arbitrarily who do you look to to answer a question, but when it is consistently anybody but me, it makes me feel left out."

Alice agreed. "You'd think by now my husband and I would have perfected coping skills. Not a bit! Someone from the family calls, one of our two boys, [and] has a long talk with my husband. At the end I say, 'What did they say, what did they say? Tell me what they said.' 'Oh, nothing, really, it wasn't, there was nothing there, they just went on talking.'"

"How true, how true," Walt said. "My wife will talk to one of the boys somewhere around the country for fifteen minutes and I say, 'What did he say?' 'He said, Hi.'"

Yet the biggest problem threatening family relations, Village SHHH members believed, was others' belief that the hard-of-hearing person used his or her hearing loss selectively.

"He turns his aids off and just doesn't listen," a colleague in my department complained about his father. "I'd like to do that. Shut it out!"

"Common misconceptions?" Ann asked. "I'm sure you share with me people who have said to you, 'Oh, she hears when she *wants* to.'"

"Yes!" Susan answered. "I was with a friend this week and I couldn't understand what she was saying and I asked her to repeat it and she got real angry at me and said, 'Why don't you *listen*!'"

Ann compared others' expectation that hard-of-hearing people "open up their ears and hear" to expecting someone in a wheelchair "to get out of the wheelchair and walk up the stairs." She pleaded with family members for consideration: "We're not just being mean, or hard to get along with. We can't understand. We just didn't get it. We can't hear!"

Yet, Ann went on to explain, there is the very real phenomenon that hard-of-hearing people hear well sometimes and poorly at others. This makes it seem that they sometimes don't want to hear. "Some day you could be in the same room and yet you don't hear as well. That could be because you're tired from the day before, you had to listen so hard. You just can't put the emotional energy into listening. Could be there's an air conditioner on today. Could be somebody scratching the table."

"There are forty reasons" hard-of-hearing people hear sometimes but not at others, Dr. Samuel Trychin said during the workshop some of us attended in 1996. "If I talk to Howard from two feet away at this volume level, he understands me. But if I move four feet away"—Dr. Trychin took a step back from the tall man in the second row—"my voice is not half as loud, it's one-eighth as loud. That can be very confusing to a family member if you're standing in the kitchen talking, and we answer back and forth, and I move over here and he's talking the same way and I'm not getting it. He'll think I'm not paying attention, I'm not interested in what he's saying—that's his interpretation. But it's the distance."

Other barriers to hearing are even more subtle. "For example, if I say to you, 'It's time to go to sleep,'" Dr. Trychin emphasized the high pitch of the word "sleep," "you may have trouble understanding me. But if I say, 'It's time to go to bed,' a nice low-frequency word, you'll hear it. If I don't understand that you hear some sounds but not others, I can think you have 'selective hearing' and that you're ignoring me."

To compound the situation, hard-of-hearing people are most likely to miss family members' first words or changes in topic. As Maggie explained during a chapter meeting, "Successful communication is aided by our ability to predict a response." Yet who can predict when someone will change the subject or first start to talk?

"I get most of what my husband says," Cora explained to me, as an example, "but I miss anything that's out of the blue. When I'm sitting with my husband in the car and he will just make passing remarks about something that I had no previous knowledge of, like 'See the cow,' and I have to turn around and think, 'What?'—it had no previous buildup to it, and I don't understand. I hear something, but I don't understand unless there's been, ah, this buildup to that."

Cora's example was mundane, but the problem isn't. First words frame conversations. New messages contain information that repetition doesn't. When the speaker's new words go unnoticed, everyone feels a sudden disconnection from the heart.

Village SHHH members bristled at the idea that they don't listen. But they also complained that one of the reasons they don't hear well is that others don't speak well.

"When I had lunch with you and the Smiths," Abe told me in his interview, "I couldn't hear either of you."

"Either Maggie or me?" I asked. "We were too fast?"

"You were, whatever," Abe said, unwilling to press exact charges.

"But you could hear Joel," I said.

Abe paused before answering. "If he spoke slowly and clearly, yes, plus he—he had a better voice. There are a few I can think of here at [the retirement complex], and they can talk and I don't hear a word they are saying."

"Even one-on-one?" I asked. Earlier in the interview, Abe had told me that one-on-one was usually fine.

"Yeah."

"Are they women?"

"They happen to be women."

"Do they know that you don't hear them?"

"I tell them."

"But they keep talking anyway," I say with a nervous laugh, realizing that "those women" now included me.

In fact, hard-of-hearing people talk about hearing a daughter but not a sister-in-law; a friend but not a son; one member of a group but not another. Most see the problem as a misfit between their hearing loss and the other person's volume or pitch. For example, men generally speak about an octave lower than women—a small difference but enough to give men's words more resonance.

During one meeting when Martha told Cassie she hadn't been able to hear her, Walt commented, "It's the frequency. She's got a very soft voice, and it's high pitched. I can see her mouth move, but that's all."

Yet other members believed that mishearing can suggest other problems—more social than physical. "My whole family!" Bob said in exasperation. "They can't learn no matter what you tell them. I have a friend named Mary who was with me, and my boy said, 'Why do you understand her all the time but you can't tell what I'm saying?'"

Bob's comment suggests that being able to understand a person may sometimes depend on the quality or familiarity of the relationship. For example, my husband's father understood my husband on the telephone but not me. Yet my father could usually understand me but not my husband.

In part, these experiences may reflect the extent of familiarity with the other person's speech habits and voice. As Dee once said about her husband, Ted, "I know his voice, phrases, so well I can hear him even if I can't hear him."

I asked Abe if his hearing loss had been very bad when his wife was living.

"I had problems. It's hard to answer. I don't know," he said.

"Did it interfere with your talking with her, having conversations with her?"

"Not that I remember."

"She didn't say anything to you about your not listening or anything like that?"

"No. She had a good voice. She knew that I, that I had problems."

What do hard-of-hearing people view as a good voice? As Abe implied, it is the voice of a person who knows about the other's hearing problem and accommodates it. "Now when my daughter calls," Susan said, "I can understand her clearly. She speaks slowly and a little loud. And I know what she is saying. But with my sister-in-law, I don't even try. . . . If I ask her to repeat, she just says the same thing over again just as fast, so I let it go."

A year after I interviewed her, Laura reported a breakthrough in her family. Until that point, she'd had a hard time getting her family to take her hearing loss seriously. She smiled with excitement as she announced the breakthrough to the group. "At least one member of my family has finally caught onto the fact that I don't hear well. My one, my first son, who I only see a couple times a year, when he calls, he speaks very slowly. He says all his words have to have a space between them so I can be sure to hear. It hasn't worked for the rest of my family."

For all of us, some voices come through loud and clear

while others remain muffled and indistinct. How much of this can be explained by the physiology of hearing loss and the clarity of speech, and how much by relations of familiarity and caring?

Tips for Family Members

There are several practical ways to improve communication in family settings.

Get Close

"Look at the person," Abe said during a chapter meeting at which we discussed hearing loss among family members. "That's as much help as whether the hard-of-hearing person is using a hearing aid or not."

"Get my attention. Let me see your face—these two things are critical," Dr. Trychin listed the first two rules for communicating with a hard-of-hearing person. "When they don't happen, we have all kinds of communication problems. Yet it's very difficult to remember that. I'm in the kitchen doing dishes and I want to talk to you. Well, it's hard for me to remember to stop what I'm doing in the kitchen, dry my hands off, walk to where you are, and get your attention and talk to you. And it's much more difficult to remember that if you talk to me when I'm in the kitchen. So to do this right, we have to have a rule that says, whoever initiates the conversation goes to where the other person is."

"We have clear communication rules in my home," a young woman agreed. "You can't scream from another room to get someone's attention. You have to come into the room where I am. My husband will still say, 'But I told you that. Didn't you hear me?' And I say, 'Did I say yes or no? If not, I didn't hear you.'"

Mark Transitions

Since first words and changes of subject are hard to predict and easy to miss, communication improves when speakers announce their changes in subject. At chapter meetings, for example, people usually said "I have a question" before they asked it, and identified topics before talking about them. During a discussion of communication struggles in the family, Alice raised the possibility of making this contexting more systematic: "I just thought of a new idea—I haven't tried it—when you get to where the conclusion is, say, maybe, 'Conclusion.' Maybe work this out ahead of time. Say 'Subject' and then I will get the subject, usually. I miss the name, I miss the change of subjects, so I miss key things. Subject, conclusion, or the action, the verb. Those three things are the chief things to zoom in on, aren't they?"

Bob agreed that it would help if everyone provided this kind of linguistic framing. "Very often it would be helpful," he said, "if my partner would turn to me and say, 'We're talking about the trip to Chicago.' When I know that, I can put it all together; I can tell what they're saying. But I have to know what the subject is, whether it [has to do with] yesterday, or today, or tomorrow."

"This is where we get lost a lot," Dr. Trychin said. "You're talking about the movie *Star Wars* and, all of a sudden, without telling me, you say, 'Did you see the new car wash down the street?' And I'm going star wars, car wars, car wars down the street? No! You have to say, 'I'm not talking about the movie now; I want to talk about the new car wash down the street.'"

Create Turns

Overlapping words and simultaneous talk are part of many people's styles of conversation (Tannen 1994). But when one person is hard of hearing, this style of conversing can rob that person of the chance to talk. One solution is to be conscious of taking turns.

When we met in the lobby to discuss our concerns as family members, Opal asked Tom how he and Ann handled conversation within their household. "What we've worked out at home," Tom answered, "is that when speaking, stand up. The kids had to learn this, too."

Opal was aghast. "Doesn't that inhibit the spontaneity," she asked.

"It enhances respect," Tom answered. "At our dining table, we had to change. Ann can't be part of dinner if we don't act this way. No one speaks until the other is done. Don't interrupt."

Tom and Ann were not the only self-help group members I met who restructured family conversation to enhance equality of participation. When Ted and Dee gave a presentation to the group, they deliberately took turns using a single mike. "If you were both hearing," one member observed, "you would use both mikes and speak at the same time."

Cora's husband agreed. "We talk simultaneously," he said.

"That's the problem," Ted said.

"Don't you do that?" someone asked.

"I have to focus too hard on hearing to speak at the same time," Dee answered.

"When I'm in an argument and both of us are talking," Ted said, "I let part of it go, catch phrases. In our relationship, I want to listen actively. Whenever I don't, that's where conflict arises."

Don't Rely on Another's Ears

Dee's hearing deteriorated early in her marriage; now, forty years later, Ted's hearing was failing. For all their emphasis on equality, they were discovering how much Dee had come to rely on Ted to be her ears.

"Since I started having significant difficulty with hearing," Dee confessed to Ted in a "couple dialogue" in front of the group, "you have been my ears. Now that you are losing more of your hearing, I experience almost fury."

Ted nodded but also expressed pain. "I have the feeling that once you depend on me as your hearing dog, hearing person, it becomes difficult to reverse roles."

I saw Dee at a banquet a year later. Illness had kept Ted from attending, but Dee was there to deliver the speech Ted wrote from his hospital bed. As Dee moved toward the podium, a real hearing dog walked by her side.

Sarah's younger sister communicated largely by sign. When she was eight years old and didn't want to hear, she put her hands over her eyes. Hard-of-hearing people sometimes complain that their partners do the same when they turn their heads during conversation or walk away. To share words and meanings, to share lives, people must work at staying in each other's presence.

Even in the most sympathetic families, people speak from other rooms or look away while talking. As Samuel Trychin emphasizes in his workshops, we do this not because we are bad but because, in the enthusiasm of the moment, we forget. Yet, however understandable, our lapses produce pain and distance. Improving communication requires that we make the changes that keep communication channels open. We need to come into each other's presence before we speak, invite and demarcate turns, use framing words, and give each other visual and oral feedback.

Communication involves more than talking and listening. It also involves a conscious effort to bridge the distance between us. This is sometimes hardest to do within the family, where we take our common ground for granted. Family members who angrily ask "Why don't you listen?" express the pain of the severed union. Loved ones who plead "We just didn't get it" are asking for yet another chance to unite through talk.

11

Across the
Generations

On a sunny morning four years after joining Village SHHH, I received a call from Marie, the cheerful woman who stepped down as chapter secretary the day I joined. Marie still came to chapter meetings occasionally; sometimes our paths crossed in town or on campus. More often, I saw her out walking with her husband, Chase. An athletic, white-haired couple, they moved down the sidewalk at a brisk pace.

Marie called to tell me that her oldest daughter, Shana, was in town. A graduate student in clinical psychology, Shana was beginning her dissertation research on growing up with deaf parents. "I think you two should get together," Marie said.

The next morning, Shana and I sat in armchairs in her parents' living room, comparing our experiences as daughters of hard-of-hearing/deaf fathers. I was grateful for another daughter's perspective. Shana's experience seemed richer, more complex than mine. My father did not always hear me clearly. Shana's father never heard her voice at all. With her training in clinical psychology, she also raised questions that I had never thought of.

Before our meeting, Shana had read a draft of some early writing I shared with the self-help group, which her mother, Marie, had sent to her. Shana saw her father as occupying a more marginal social space than Village SHHH members, as less fully a part of the hearing world.

"My father doesn't belong to the Deaf world, or to the hearing world," Shana said soon after we sat down to talk. "And we got a bit of this alienation."

Shana felt her early years to be quite normal. Her father made a good living for them as a technical writer, took her and her sisters to art galleries, and read bedtime stories. Despite their father's deafness, their house was not quiet. It was filled with four girls' laughter, their dancing, their mother's piano playing.

It was in adolescence that Shana began to feel her family was different. Spending the day with friends, she observed the ease with which some girls talked to their fathers. At these girls' birthday parties, they watched American movies, not the subtitled foreign films her family saw. "I had always seen my father as special," Shana summed up. "Then I began to see him as different."

In my four years with Village SHHH, I never saw Shana's father at a chapter meeting. According to Marie, Chase heard too little to get anything from them. Except for Maggie, who continued attending off and on after Joel could not, she was the only hearing spouse to do so.

"You see," Marie explained later when she joined Shana and me in the living room, "the grandparents were wonderful people, salt of the earth, but when Shana's father lost his hearing [from spinal meningitis at the age of twelve], they had no idea what to do. They were devastated, and they didn't want him to do any signing. They wanted him to belong to the hearing world. So they sent him to a lipreading school in New York City. But he was never very good at it, he says. He's had to depend on it, and it's been hard."

"You're right," Shana agreed. "I mean, from my perspective, it's through the generations, it's how his parents treated him, then how you two worked it through, and then how it got translated to us. . . . Because his parents didn't allow him to be part of the Deaf world, and even though he married a hearing woman and all his friends were hearing, you know, there's something different about him. There is something different.

"I was very touched about your writing about the punch line," Shana said, pointing to the pages of type on the table beside her. "Because that happens all the time. We'll all be sitting here laughing, and he'll be sitting here, and I think, okay, we should explain to him what was said, and then you go back and try to explain it, and the moment is lost, and he tries to laugh, and he fakes it."

"Oh, yeah," Marie said. "That drives me crazy."

"But what are you going to do?" Shana asked. "What can you do? When you've spent all the time going through the explanation, it isn't funny. It's—it's very painful."

Shana thought for a while, then began again.

"When I came here on Monday, I was really struck and disturbed by how hard it was to communicate with my father. I spent, well, pretty much all afternoon with him Monday, a long stretch of hours, and it was really—I was exhausted. I grew up doing that, and it came sort of natural for me, but when I've been away for a while, I actually found myself feeling kind of sleepy. It wasn't so much like I was bored as exhausted."

"He is exhausted, too," Marie said. "Because it's all this strain of trying to get it."

"I'm confused now because we did have a sign language in our family," Shana said, "but I don't remember how to do it."

Marie began signing the alphabet the family invented. At the letter *B*, Shana joined in.

"Yeah, *G* like that," Marie said. "I got mixed up."

"*H*," Shana continued, and together, they signed to *L*.

In graduate school, Shana enrolled in a class to learn American Sign Language.

"On the first night, they gave us a form and we had to put why we were there, and I put down that my father was deaf but that he had never learned to sign, and I really wanted to learn it. And I was so—I was so ostracized by the teacher, who was a Deaf woman. . . .

"For the last class, she went out of the room, and when she came back, she accused me of talking. We weren't allowed to talk from the moment we got there till the class was over. And I said in sign to her that I hadn't been, and the whole class stuck up for me. . . . Later, I put two and two together, and I thought that it must have had something to do with that initial thing—that my father had never learned to sign, was oral."

"You feel she resented you because your father was not part of her culture?" I asked.

"And he could have been. And I was waiting until age thirty-something to join it."

As Shana spoke, her father's dependence on lipreading became subtly apparent. Shana's hands flew; her mouth moved more slowly. "Body English," Marie commented. "You learn to mold things with your mouth, carefully."

"I've gotten away from it considerably," Shana said, "but I used to use my hands all the time to talk to people, and I probably did a lot of grimacing. People still say I sometimes make a lot of facial expressions that are not so attractive, but that are, I think, from that." She demonstrated with masks of tragedy and comedy. The grandparents' decision had become part of her body.

Shana has begun to see more and more connections between her father's deafness and her present reality. "It's interesting," she said. "I've always had boyfriends who've had some impairment. My husband, John, can't hear in one ear. And the boyfriend I had before my husband had a stutter, another communication difficulty. I remember thinking at the time, isn't this interesting—what am I doing?

"And yet, I honestly forget about John's hearing. I'm not very sensitive at all to his hearing. And he's usually angry with me, at certain times, when, you know, he can't hear me. . . . And he accuses me of anger, about how I get really angry with him when he can't hear something I've said. I think, what kind of anger do I hold at my father not being able to hear me? What kind of anger have I repressed? And I also think I have a thing about other people hearing me, in general. I get really nuts when I think people don't understand me, or can't hear me."

"Or don't listen to what you're saying," Marie interjected.

"Right. Well, I don't know that it's that they don't listen," Shana answered. "I think it's that they don't hear what I'm saying, which is sort of deeper to me. They don't get what I'm saying, they don't understand it. And I really have to watch myself, especially with men. If they can't hear me, or if I feel like they don't understand me, it just drives me crazy."

Shana traced this anger back to her early years. "You know," she said, "we used to really be terrible when my mother went out. She didn't go out very often, but choir practice or something, and Dad would be left to watch us, and every time she went out, we were so bad—we would jump on the bed. We would, we'd have this pillow fight! We were so noisy, and what he would do is, he could hear the vibration, and he would come in and always made us feel, ughhh, just so terrible. I mean, 'cause he would say, 'I guess you don't think I know what's going on? You're taking advantage of me.'"

"He did?" Marie asked. "I never knew this!"

"Sometimes he'd open the door—we wouldn't hear him coming because he was soft, you know, everything about him is kind of soft—and we'd be in there, boing, boing, BOING, CRASH! And he really got upset with that, and we usually felt pretty bad about it."

Shana paused. "It was also a rebellion."

"It was a rebellion," Marie said. "Against both of us. Against me, because I left you, and against him, because he couldn't hear."

After talking to Shana, I asked myself about similar episodes, about latent anger. I found none I could immediately trace to hearing loss. I don't remember becoming aware of my father's hearing problem until sometime in my teens when I saw a government check made out in his name. It was a small check—$30?—monthly compensation for the hearing disability he acquired during World War II. Dad rarely talked about the war years, never about the hearing loss. Dad lost his hearing, Mom told me, from serving in Europe during all the bombing—at the age of thirty-five, one of the oldest men to be drafted and shipped overseas.

While I was growing up, Dad drove a truck for a local wholesale company. Like many other working-class men of his generation, he worked long hours and came home tired, often beginning the evening meal as the rest of us were finishing up. Later he read the newspaper or dozed off on the couch, waking to catch the 11 o'clock news. Shana recalls her deaf father's overwhelming presence, but I ache with my hard-of-hearing father's puzzling absence.

It's hard to separate the effects of Dad's hearing from all the other influences—his Finnish stoicism, his working-class fatigue. Yet I'm beginning to think that Dad's hearing loss played a larger part in our household than I had imagined, a corner piece in the puzzle of family life.

I asked my brother what he remembers. At the age of eight or ten, Matt recalled, Mom asked him to wake Dad, telling him to shake Dad because he usually slept on his "good ear." About the same time, Matt became aware of how Dad looked when he was talking to the other men at church. Standing in the circle, Dad leaned forward and tilted his head, straining to keep up with every word. Within the family, Dad tuned out conversation more than he leaned in.

By the time Dad finally got a hearing aid, at the age of seventy, he had lost a lot more of his hearing. With Dad in the background, I spoke to my mother. She relayed information and decisions from Dad.

Marie also relays information within her family.

"I was very touched last night when my sister called," Shana told Marie near the end of our conversation. "How, after you got off the phone, you came and sat on that footstool, and you very quietly told him that conversation, and the two of you talked about it. I was touched about that because I have this perception that I talk to my mother and then my father doesn't get that information."

"Oh," Marie replied. "He gets it."

"And you took all that time with him," Shana said, "and

sometimes I wonder how hard it must be for you that you have to be the go-between from us to him."

Marie had always done extra work to include Chase. "You know," she said, "I very seldom—I can't think of anything that I do that's major that I don't ask him what he thinks about it. I don't walk all over him at all, I sure don't, and that's partly—he's old-fashioned in a lot of this. But I feel this—that because he's deaf, he needs the self-confidence that a wife will say to him, you know, what about this? . . . I think in any decision about the kids at all, it was always, we always got together on that. He usually ruled, too," she shook her head for emphasis.

In our parents' generation, people expected the man to have the say. In serving as their husband' ears and mouths, our mothers underwrote our fathers' roles as patriarchs.

Is there anything about our fathers' hearing loss that makes Shana and me our fathers' daughters?

"I don't know whether you know this," Marie said to Shana about her hospitalization ten years before, "but before I came out of the anesthetic, the surgeon told Chase, you know, wrote it down, what it was, and he went—you know I wouldn't be back in my room, conscious, for a while—and he went to the library like that and he read up everything he could possibly find on that. That was always the way he did things. If he wanted to know what something was, he researched it."

Shana's research today mirrors her father's. She has returned to graduate school for the Ph.D.

What do I carry from my father?

After Mom died, Dad seldom traveled outside the neighborhood, yet he made frequent trips to the public library. Entering the house after Dad died, I saw the papers and books just as he left them, stacked on tables and beside his chair. I found a note in his handwriting on the dining room table with the name of a book he planned to get.

When I interview SHHH members, I see the same thing—books and newspapers everywhere. I wonder if this is the result of their mostly middle-class status, or compensation for gaps in the spoken word.

In her family, Marie tells me, all the daughters write, following Chase's lead as a technical writer.

"That is Chase's strong point, even today. If I have an important letter to write, I put it all down on paper and I say to Chase, do something with this, and he is expert at this. The oldest daughter is an English teacher; Shana has done a lot of medical writing; Ann teaches science. . . ."

"She's also, I mean, she's published a lot," Shana interrupts. "She's really a writer as well."

"And Janie works for the government, interpreting coding."

"So, I guess you are all writers and, I guess, readers?" I ask.

"Oh, readers, yeah," Marie answers.

Chase carries a notepad so that others can write to him.

"As you can see," Marie waves at the paintings stacked around the room, "Chase takes art classes over at the university. The professor . . . will say the most awful things to him, and Chase knows how to take it; he just loves it. And [the teacher] writes to him; he wants him to know what's going on, he puts it down on paper, even his jokes. Chase will come home; he's got this piece of paper with a joke on it.

"Chase has always been interested in art, and he has read, and he's gone to all the museums, all the shows, and the professor will say, 'This looks like de Kooning,' and he

knows that Chase will immediately know what he's getting at."

Marie remembers back to Shana's growing-up years.
"You kids grew up with art. . . . On Sunday afternoons, we'd
go into the Corcoran, or the Phelps Gallery, or the National
Museum. . . . But also, this is the thing, I think all of you
remember that he read to you, every evening. I mean, this
was his job. I don't like to read out loud very much, but he
would, and I would hear him in there—'Dr. Goat put on
his coat.' He had a rather soft voice, but because he heard at
one time, he has inflection. And he would imitate all the
voices. . . . I could see these little kids in their nighties, all
sitting next to him, and they were always wiggling, you
know, like this, and he was sitting there reading all this stuff
in all the different voices."

Shana puts on her deepest voice. "And Doctor Goat put
on his coat." Shana and Marie laugh with pleasure.

Did Dad ever read to me? Looking back at my relationship with my father feels like searching through Lake Erie's
gray stones for wave-polished glass. I locate a few shiny moments with Dad in the early years—seated at the drugstore
for a fountain coke at age seven, him holding the big bike
steady for me at age eight, in a fishing boat with Matt at age
thirteen, watching me from his delivery truck as I led children in games at an inner-city park, age nineteen. Could
he have known then how precious those moments are to
me now?

Then there is the long stretch of years with few memories. After I finished college, Dad and I saw each other
briefly during the summers and Christmas breaks. Mom and
I talked and visited while Dad kept busy with reading and
chores. Was my father's busyness an emotional retreat—not

being seen, he didn't have to worry about having to re-
spond, or trying to hear? Dad's frequent silences left a feeling of distance.

After getting the hearing aid, Dad went through a small
social renaissance. He became, as Matt put it, "a bit more of
a conversationalist." Then Mom was gone and Dad was
alone. When I called, I waited for Dad to answer the phone.
Although our talks left precious memories, they couldn't
make up for the quiet years. Who was the person at the
other end of the line? I long to have better known my
father.

Families are social systems. What's going on with one
member affects all. Families are also patterns of relationship
we take for granted and have a hard time seeing.

Shana and I may wonder how family life might have
been different if our fathers—and Shana's grandparents—
had responded to our fathers' hearing loss differently. What
if Shana's father had learned to sign? Or if mine got a hearing aid in his forties, instead of his seventies? These are
questions that we, of course, can't answer. Yet I believe that
if our stories have a common point, it's this: The choices of
one generation set the pattern for the weavings of the next.

Postscript

I'd spent an enjoyable hour sipping coffee and grading final exams at Café Trio. Crossing the street to campus, a journalism professor I knew caught up with me. "Are you through grading?" I asked, using my chin to point to the papers overflowing my arms.

"No," he shook his head. "I taught editing this semester—no final exam. But I do have sixty-five teacher articles to review for a newspaper contest." He shrugged his shoulders and rolled his eyes.

"Teacher articles," I said, "About teachers?"

He looked surprised. "Not teachers," he said. "Features."

He went on talking as if nothing had happened. But inside I was making a mental note. I'd learned at SHHH meetings that this was the classic kind of hearing error. I got the vowels but missed the consonant.

A few days later, I was in the doctor's office for a fiftieth-year physical exam. Filling out the screening form in the waiting room, I came to the section on hearing and vision. On the line for "hearing problems," I skipped the boxes for yes and no and wrote in "maybe."

An hour later, the nurse, a petite older woman with curly white hair, announced that she'd be giving me a hearing test. Susan carried in a box the size of a large handbag. "You probably remember this from grade school," she said as she handed me the headphones. I watched her plug in the box, then took the signaling device she handed me.

"Turn around," Susan admonished. "I don't like people to watch when I'm turning the knobs."

I closed my eyes and tried to breathe slowly. For what seemed like forever, all I heard was the hallway traffic and the buzzing lights overhead. Finally, I heard a faint tone. Oh, that's what I'm listening for, I thought, and pressed the red button.

The hearing test lasted about ten minutes. Beginning with low pitches, the tone shifted gradually to the treble clef. But the tones didn't seem to come evenly. Sometimes I waited and waited. Other times I pressed the red button quickly. I was never quite sure—was I hearing a tone or making it up? It crossed my mind that Susan was trying to trick me. I don't want to fail this test, I thought. And, yet, if I don't hear well, won't that be interesting?

"Okay, we're done," Susan said abruptly, and reached for the headphones.

"But how did I do?" I asked.

"It does look like there's some loss at the upper end," she answered, looking down. She handed me the filled-in audiogram.

The *X*s and *O*s proceeded together across the left side of the chart, then dipped abruptly mid-graph.

"You can leave now," Susan said, retrieving the audiogram. "It's been twenty minutes since the tetanus shot."

"But I want to talk to the doctor," I said. I couldn't believe she was dismissing me without any discussion.

A few minutes later, Dr. Mann's tall frame leaned into the room. "Why are you still here?"

"I wanted you to look at my audiogram."

Dr. Mann took the audiogram out of the chart and studied it briefly.

"You probably have some trouble hearing women," he commented. "You should be fine hearing Majid."

"But sometimes I don't hear him," I said. "I also have trouble hearing students when they talk from the back of the class."

"Were you exposed to loud noise when you were younger?" he asked. "Work construction? Play music?"

I was always in the orchestra," I answered. "I play violin."

"Orchestras can get pretty loud," he commented. "Do you play now?"

"Yes." How could I tell him that music is one of my dearest pleasures? Would I begin to lose that?

"You could wear earplugs," the doctor's voice brought me back. "No, I guess you really need to hear the others when you play." He frowned a moment, then smiled. "I know a man who wears two hearing aids and plays in a band. He even travels with them."

A few minutes later, Susan walked over to me as I was writing the check to pay the bill. "What did Dr. Mann say about the audiogram?" she asked.

"He's referred me to the university audiology clinic," I said, a copy of the audiogram in my hand.

"What can they do?" she said. "You're too young to wear hearing aids."

Six years of SHHH meetings ran through my head. If I need them, I thought, I'll get behind-the-ear hearing aids with a telecoil. Maybe I should get them in fluorescent!

I occasionally got out my audiogram and studied it. There was that precipitous drop at 3,000 Hz. Had our neighborhood been noisier than I remembered? Did Dad's hearing loss have a hereditary component?

The next month, at the audiology clinic, I followed Dr.

Taborn down the hall and into a testing room. Seated across from me in a swivel chair, our knees almost touching, he looked me in the eye and asked what brought me there.

"I have trouble hearing my students."

"How large of a class?" Dr. Taborn asked, his eyebrows raised.

"Eighty last semester, fifty this, but now I'm in a room with overhead vents that make a lot of noise."

"Do you hear better with one ear than the other?"

That's an interesting question, I thought, then laughed. I was offering him my left ear.

Dr. Taborn conducted the hearing tests from the room directly behind me. In the first test, Dr. Taborn asked me to repeat the words I heard. "Sidewalk." "Playground." "Baseball." After a while, the silences between words grew longer.

The second test was the same one Susan gave me, with pure tones repeated at successively higher frequency intervals. Finally, Dr. Taborn did a test for conductive hearing loss. To test for this less common type of hearing loss, he angled a special headset into position—not on the ears but against the bone behind one ear and in front of the other.

When we finished the tests, Dr. Taborn returned with the clipboard, turning it around so the audiogram faced in my direction. "Zero decibels is excellent," he said, pointing to the top. "Normal adult hearing is between 0 and 20 decibels."

I looked. The audiogram was very similar to the one I had brought home from the doctor's office. For both ears, the response curve tracked somewhat evenly at about 15 dB across the top of the chart, then dropped to 30 dB at

3,000 Hz, and then down to 50 dB (left ear) and 70 dB (right ear) at 6,000 Hz. The audiogram is reproduced as figure 1.

"As for the cause," Dr. Taborn continued, "if you were seventy, I would say it's associated with aging. But since you're fifty, I'd have to say the etiology is unknown. It could be noise induced. It could have been medication you took for some illness. It could have been some trauma to the head."

"Could I have had it for a while?"

"Yes. It could have happened in your teenage years. And it could get worse quickly. You need to come back in two years, or sooner if you notice a difference. Right now, your loss is not one that a hearing aid can help."

"What am I missing?" I asked.

"With background noise, the *th*s, the *t*s, *s*s, silent *th*s. Numbers may be difficult. You may miss the plural *s* at the end of words. Your number-one enemy is environmental noise. In noisy situations, people lean more on the higher frequencies, but you can't rely on those sounds."

Dr. Taborn went on to assure me that since there is a lot of redundancy in speech, in good conditions I should have few problems.

A "small" hearing loss, I thought. I recalled an exchange an SHHH member reported to Rocky Stone, the organization's national founder. "I told Rocky I had a small hearing loss," the member said. "There are no small hearing losses," Stone responded (Stone 1990: 25).

"Is there anything you can recommend for me to read?" I asked Dr. Taborn. I thought I'd seen most of the books out there, but maybe there was a book I had overlooked.

"Well, you could read about the psychology of it, how to cope. You might watch to see how you are coping. Of course, you should try to sit in a quiet place in restaurants. And I think you should really try to get a different classroom."

When I joined Village SHHH, members spoke about Dr. Taborn as their favorite audiologist. He is warm, personable, matter of fact. Still, I left his office with only the most rudimentary advice: no book titles, no explanation of assistive listening devices, and no mention of a self-help group like SHHH. But, to be fair, even with all that I supposedly "knew," I had asked few questions. Like Walt, I had sat there silent.

At Village SHHH, I've occasionally heard someone say, "I bet many of us know more than our audiologists." In reference to medical and technical matters, that's certainly not true. But in understanding and fleshing out the life issues involved, it often is. That's why groups like SHHH and ALDA really matter.

The loss of hearing sets a person on a new life journey. When people become hard of hearing, they find they have to steer through many curves and tight spaces of miscommunication. Ready or not, co-workers, family, and friends are along for the ride. Yet with work and the help of those who've gone before, it may be possible to avoid some of the roadblocks. This book, I hope, gives a bit of a roadmap.

References

Bakke, Matthew H. 1995. "Hearing Aids and the Consumer: An Overview of Current Hearing Aid Wisdom." *SHHH Journal* 16 (3): 13–17.

Barr, Norman Lee, Jr. 1996. "Tinnitus, or Head Noises" (brochure). Washington, D.C.: Better Hearing Institute.

Compton, Cynthia L. 1989. *Assistive Devices: Doorways to Independence*. Washington, D.C.: Gallaudet University.

Dugan, Marcia B. 1997. *Keys to Living with Hearing Loss*. Hauppauge, N.Y.: Barron's.

Edwards, Betty. 1989. *Drawing on the Right Side of the Brain*. Los Angeles: Tarcher.

Gantz, Bruce J. 1992. "Cochlear Implants for Children." *SHHH Journal* 13 (6): 30–31.

Gates, G. A., et al. "Hearing in the Elderly: The Framingham Cohort, 1983–1985. Pt. I. Basic Audiometric Test Results." *Ear and Hearing* 11: 247–56.

Gordon-Salant, Sandra. 1990. "Special Amplification Considerations for Elderly Individuals." In *The Vanderbilt Hearing Aid Report II*, edited by Gerald A. Studebaker, Fred H. Bess, and Lucile B. Beck. Parkton, Md.: York Press.

Gurevitch, Z. D. 1989. "Distance and Conversation." *Symbolic Interaction* 12 (2): 251–63.

Hazell, Jonathan W. P. 1995. "Models of Tinnitus: Generation, Perception, Clinical Implications." In *Mechanisms of Tinnitus*, edited by Jack A. Vernon and Aage R. Moller. Boston: Allyn and Bacon.

Mehan, Hugh, and Houston Wood. 1975. *Reality of Ethnomethodology*. New York: Wiley.

Meikle, Mary B. 1995. "The Interaction of Central and Peripheral Mechanisms in Tinnitus." In *Mechanisms of Tinnitus*, edited by Jack A. Vernon and Aage R. Moller. Boston: Allyn and Bacon.

Northern, Jerry L., and Marion P. Downs. 1991. *Hearing in Children*. 4ᵗʰ ed. Baltimore: Williams and Wilkins.

Pope, Anne. In collaboration with Self Help for Hard of Hearing People. 1997. *Hear: Solutions, Skills, and Sources for People with Hearing Loss*. New York: Dorling Kindersley.

Roeser, Ross J. 1994. "Cochlear Implant Choices: A Look at Three Manufacturers." *SHHH Journal* 15 (3): 31–33.

Ross, Mark. 1997. "Digital Hearing Aids: An Update." *Hearing Loss* 18 (5): 8–15.

———. 1998. "Developments in Research and Technology." *Hearing Loss* 19 (5): 32–34.

Sacks, Harvey. 1974. "An Analysis of the Course of a Joke's Telling in Communication." In *Explorations in the Ethnography of Speaking,* edited by Richard Bauman and Joel Sherzer. Cambridge: Cambridge University Press.

Self Help for Hard of Hearing People, Inc. n.d. "Hearing Loss: You Can Do Something about It!" (brochure). Bethesda, Md.: SHHH Publications.

Stone, Howard E. "Rocky." 1990. *An Invisible Condition: The Human Side of Hearing Loss.* Bethesda, Md.: SHHH Publications.

Tannen, Deborah. 1994. *Gender and Discourse.* New York: Oxford University Press.

Tucker, Bonnie Poitras. 1995. *The Feel of Silence.* Philadelphia: Temple University Press.

Vernon, Jack A., and Aage R. Moller. 1995. *Mechanisms of Tinnitus.* Boston: Allyn and Bacon.

Wardhaugh, Ronald. 1993. *Investigating Language: Central Problems in Linguistics.* Oxford: Blackwell.

Yellin, M. Wende, and Peter S. Roland. 1997. "Special Auditory/Vestibular Testing." In *Hearing Loss,* edited by Peter S. Roland, Bradley F. Marple, and William L. Meyerhoff. New York: Thieme.

Selected List
of Resources

Self-Help Groups
SHHH

Self Help for Hard of Hearing People, Inc. (SHHH) has affiliates in forty-nine states and Canada. To locate the chapter or group nearest you, contact:

> Self Help for Hard of Hearing People, Inc.
> 7910 Woodmont Avenue, Suite 1200
> Bethesda, MD 20814
> (301) 657-2248 (voice)
> (301) 657-2249 (TTY)
> FAX: (301) 913-9413
> E-mail: national@shhh.org
> Website: www.shhh.org

A few state and chapter associations post information about their groups and activities on the Web. E-mail addresses as of July 1998 are as follows:

> California SHHH: www.shhhca.org
>
> North Carolina SHHH: www.geocities.com/Heartland/Prairie/ 4727
>
> Derbytown, Kentucky, SHHH: www/geocities.com/Heartland/ Plains/5958/shhh.html
>
> Montgomery County, Maryland, SHHH: members.tripod.com/ ~maf_/mcshhh

Beyond-Hearing

Beyond-Hearing (BH) is an Internet e-mail list run from the Duke University Academic Computing Center. Co-founded by Miriam (Mimi) Clifford (dmimi@duke.edu) and Dana Mulvany, Beyond-Hearing is "in-

125

tended to provide a communication vehicle for people who have a hearing loss and who seek to overcome the barriers of hearing loss between themselves, other people, and the environment."

Many BH subscribers are experts in the field of hearing loss, either by profession or experience. Others are newcomers who tell their stories and solicit and receive advice. In recent months, topics on BH have included how to hook up an ALD in a car; what medications may cause hearing loss; and how hearing loss may affect concentration.

To subscribe to Beyond-Hearing, send an e-mail message to major-domo@duke.edu. Use no subject line. Type the following message, exactly as is, on the first line of the message body:

> subscribe beyond-hearing

To send a message to the list, e-mail to: beyond-hearing@duke.edu.

ALDA

The Association of Late Deafened Adults (ALDA) is a self-help organization for people who have lost their hearing after the development of speech. The organization was founded in Chicago in 1987.

> Association of Late Deafened Adults, Inc.
> 10310 Main Street, Box 274
> Fairfax, VA 22030
> (404) 289-1596 (TTY)
> FAX: (404) 284-6862
> Website: www.alda.org

IFHOH

The International Federation of Hard of Hearing People (IFHOH) maintains a Website with links to other national organizations that serve hard-of-hearing people.

> Website: www.ifhoh.org

Alexander Graham Bell Association

The Alexander Graham Bell Association for the Deaf is a membership organization with twenty-nine chapters in the United States and Canada. The focus of the association is on oral methods of communication. The association has three hundred book titles available and also produces and disseminates brochures and pamphlets.

Alexander Graham Bell Association for the Deaf
3417 Volta Place N.W.
Washington, D.C. 20007
(202) 337-8767 (Publications Department)
(202) 337-5220 (V/TTY)
E-mail: agbell2@aol.com
Website: www.agbell.org

Help with Hearing Aids

The first step in being fitted for amplification is to get your hearing tested. The following two organizations maintain lists of certified audiologists:

American Speech-Language-Hearing Association
10801 Rockville Pike
Rockville, MD 20852
(800) 638-TALK (V/TTY)

American Academy of Audiology
8201 Greensboro Drive, #300
McLean, VA 22102
Website: www.audiology.com

The Website for the American Academy of Audiology has an extensive "Consumer Resources" section that includes "Understanding Your Audiogram," "Hearing Aids," and "Dr. Ross on Hearing Loss." Dr. Mark Ross is professor emeritus of audiology at the University of Connecticut.

In 1996, a group of scientists presented technical information on hearing and hearing aids at the SHHH convention in Orlando, Florida. This information has been gathered in book and video form. *Solutions through Science: The Latest Developments in Hearing Aid Research* is available from the Publications Department of SHHH, Inc.

Anne Pope discusses hearing aids, and how to get used to them, in her book, published in collaboration with SHHH: *Hear: Solutions, Skills, and Sources for People with Hearing Loss* (London: Dorling Kindersley, 1997; available from SHHH).

Financial Assistance

Hearing aids can be expensive. The following organizations may be able to provide financial assistance, in some cases:

HEAR NOW
9745 E. Hampden Avenue, Suite 300
Denver, CO 80231-4923
(303) 695-7797 (V/TTY); (800) 648-HEAR
FAX: (303) 695-7789
E-mail: 107737.1272@compuserve.com
Website: www.leisurelan.com/hearnow

SERTOMA International Foundation
9745 East Meyer Boulevard
Kansas City, MO 64132
(816) 333-8300 (voice/TTY)

Veterans Administration (VA) Audiology and Speech
Pathology Services
50 Irving Street NW
Washington, DC 20422
(202) 745-8270 (voice/TTY)

Assistive Technologies

A good place to start if you are considering using or getting an assistive device is with Cynthia Compton's book, *Assistive Devices: Doorways to Independence*. Compton shows, not just tells, the various options available for one-for-one and group interactions. An open-captioned videotape is also available. Both may be obtained from SHHH or from the Publications Department of the Alexander Graham Bell Association for the Deaf at the addresses listed under "Self-Help Groups" above.

The National Center on Assistive Technology is a program within SHHH whose goal is to raise national awareness of assistive listening technology. The center's more specific goals are to provide one-on-one assistance to audiologists and consumers in the understanding and selection of assistive devices; to train leaders in the field of assistive technologies; to produce educational materials and articles; and to inform public debate and influence policies relating to public access. A current focus is to marshal the development of cellular phone technology so as to protect the rights of hard-of-hearing consumers. The National Center on Assistive Technology can be reached through the main switchboard of SHHH, Inc., or via the fax or other addresses listed for SHHH above.

A few SHHH chapters have centers for the demonstration of assistive technologies. These centers operate one or more days per week, and members volunteer their services. Check with SHHH, Inc., to see if there is a center near you.

In the Washington, D.C., area, Gallaudet University offers demonstrations and evaluations of assistive devices through its audiology clinic but may require an appointment for an initial hearing test.

Audiology Clinic
Gallaudet University
800 Florida Ave NE
Washington, DC 20002
(202) 651-5328 (V/TTY)

The United States Architectural and Transportation Barriers Compliance Board is charged with helping employers and businesses understand and meet public-access requirements, including those for hard-of hearing and deaf people. Staff can provide technical assistance or referrals.

U.S. Architectural and Transportation Barriers Compliance
  Board
1331 F Street NW, Suite 10000
Washington, D.C. 20004-1111
(202) 272-5434 (V or TTY)

The National Institute on Disability and Rehabilitation Research, U.S. Department of Education, provides a database list of information on assistive technology and rehabilitation equipment available in the United States. ABLEDATA lists more than twenty-four thousand items of assistive technology produced by more than three thousand manufacturers. This electronic database is updated daily and includes a section devoted to assistive devices, such as hearing aids, shake awake alarms, and call-waiting signalers, for hard-of-hearing and deaf people. The database includes product information, descriptions, manufacturers' addresses, and prices but no evaluations. Inquiries may be made by e-mail, phone, fax, or in person.

ABLEDATA
8455 Colesville Road, Suite 935
Silver Spring, MD 20910
(800) 227-0216 (V); (301) 608-8912 (TTY)
FAX: (301) 608-8958
E-mail: abledata@macroint.com
Website: www.abledata.com

As a public service, SHHH member Dana Mulvany has posted on her Website a list of companies that sell "Adaptive Products for Hearing Loss" through the mail or over the Web.

members.tripod.com/~Dana_Mulvany/HOHCompanies.htm

The Telecommunications Research and Action Center and the Consumer Federation of America have a computer hotline with information about how to secure telephone equipment for hard of hearing and deaf people.

Tele-Consumer Hotline
P.O. Box 27207
Washington, D.C. 20005
www.teleconsumer.org/hotline/pubs/edpguide.html

Other Organizations and Websites
Music

"Music for All to Hear" has produced and sells a few CDs and tapes of piano and bass violin music in low frequencies, between 110 and 440 Hz. Included are childhood songs, Broadway tunes, Christmas music, and classics. For a brochure, write or call:

Music for All to Hear
P.O. Box 307331
Denton, TX 76203
(940) 591-1377

Tinnitus

The American Tinnitus Association offers brochures, a newsletter, and references regarding tinnitus research and assistance.

American Tinnitus Association
P.O. Box 5
Portland, OR 97207-0005
(503) 248-9985

Another source of information on tinnitus is:

Tinnitus and Hyperacusis Center
University of Maryland
22 South Greene Street
Baltimore, MD 21201
(800) 492-5538 (V/TTY)

Websites include:

www.cccd.edu/faq/tinnitus.html (frequently asked questions)
www.ucl.ac.uk/~rmjg101/tinnitus1.html

Captioned Films and Videos

Many captioned films and videos are available for loan free of charge to deaf and hard-of-hearing individuals and groups, as provided by funding from the U.S. Department of Education.

> Captioned Films/Videos Program
> National Association of the Deaf
> 1447 E. Main
> Spartanburg, SC 29307
> (800) 237-6213 (Voice)
> (800) 237-6819 (TTY)
> (800) 538-5636 (FAX)
> E-mail: info@cfv.org
> Website: www.cfv.org

Information about open-captioned showings of new releases may be obtained from:

> Silent Partner Interworld
> Website: www.silentpartner.org

According to its Website, "Silent Partner Interworld supports the efforts of local theaters to attract deaf audiences by providing film distribution, theater coordination, and marketing services at selected locations and theaters across the United States." The Website lists participating theaters and notes upcoming attractions.

Selected Books and Journals

Books

In the last few years, several books have come out that look at hearing loss from the inside. I've enjoyed these first-person accounts and think you will, too. Most are available from SHHH, Inc.

> Bonnie Poitras Tucker. *The Feel of Silence.* Philadelphia: Temple University Press, 1995. ISBN 1-56639-352-3.

Bonnie Poitras Tucker's hearing loss was discovered when she was two. By working at becoming an excellent lip-reader, Tucker went on to achieve success as a professor of law, a law partner, and an author. In poignant scenes and reminiscences, Tucker describes the personal and political struggles she went through to achieve these goals.

> Elaine Suss. *When the Hearing Gets Hard: Winning the Battle against Hearing Impairment.* New York: Plenum Press, 1993. ISBN 0-306-44505-0.

Elaine Suss invited her family to Thanksgiving dinner only to have her ears and hearing loss become the dinner topic. After being tested and fitted with hearing aids, Suss, a writer, decided to research and write about her experience. In a chatty, easy reading style, Suss uses anecdotes, interviews with famous and not-so-famous people, and library and original research to introduce readers to such topics as coping strategies, ALDs, and ototoxic drugs (medications that can augment or trigger hearing loss). The book includes photographs.

> Hannah Merker. *Listening: Ways of Hearing in a Silent World.* New York: HarperCollins, 1992, 1994. ISBN 0-06-017054-9.

In this lyrical memoir, Hannah Merker writes about how her life changed—and didn't change—after a skiing accident left her with a hearing loss that eventually brought her to "a silent world." Living in a houseboat on Long Island Sound, Merker, a librarian and writer, discovered new ways to hear music, friends' voices, and the sounds of nature. In her own words, "Listening becomes visual, tactile, intuitive. Listening . . . perhaps . . . is just a mind aware" (p. 17).

> Charlotte Himber. *How to Survive Hearing Loss.* Washington, D.C.: Gallaudet University Press, 1989. ISBN 0-930323-60-2.

In the midst of a yoga class, Charlotte Himber experienced a flutter of fear. She discovered that the other students had moved from lying to upright positions—only she hadn't heard the instructor's words. Charlotte Himber takes us along on her personal odyssey of denial and acceptance of her hearing loss. We sit on the bus with her as she bravely decides to remove her hearing aid from the velvet box in her purse and put it in her ear, only to have it end up dangling from the ear mold. This book is for anyone who needs to know he or she is not alone in resisting a hearing loss and in getting used to wearing—not just purchasing—a hearing aid.

> Jill Jepson, ed. *No Walls of Stone: An Anthology of Literature by Deaf and Hard of Hearing Writers.* Washington, D.C.: Gallaudet University Press, 1992. ISBN 1-56368-019-X.

In this anthology, anthropologist and linguist Jill Jepson draws together work by twenty-three contemporary deaf and hard-of-hearing writers to show how hard of hearing and deafness are "different ways of being in the world" (p. 2). In poetry, drama, short stories, and essays, contributors explore the range of emotions and sensory and interpersonal experiences of living with a hearing loss in an often "unaccommodating and aggressively hearing world" (p. 8). Some of the writings have been previously published, but most are new to this collection. Jill Jepson has a moderate hearing loss.

> Marcia B. Dugan, in collaboration with Self Help for Hard of Hearing People. *Keys to Living with Hearing Loss.* Hauppauge, N.Y.: Barron's Keys to Retirement Planning, 1997. ISBN 0-7641-0017-3.

Marcia Dugan includes a lot of information and advice, in small doses, in this book. Part of Barron's Keys to Living series, Dugan's book has forty-one short (two- to six-page) chapters ("Keys") on topics ranging from "Hearing Loss: The Early Signs" to "When Hearing Aids Are Not Enough," "Hearing in the Hospital," and "Healthy Living/Managing Stress." Appendixes list SHHH affiliates and other organizations. Although not a first-person account, this book is informed by Marcia Dugan's experience of hearing loss. Dugan is a recent past president of national SHHH.

Journals

Hearing Loss (formerly *SHHH Journal*) is the official publication of SHHH, Inc. Each issue includes regular columns by noted health professionals, featured articles on special topics (e.g., "Digital Hearing Aids: You Asked the Questions and We Found the Answers," March/April 1998), notices of current and upcoming legislation, and autobiographical and personal interest stories. Subscriptions to this bimonthly journal are included with membership in the national organization (currently $25.00, individual) and are available only to members.

Hearing Health: The Voice on Hearing Issues is a reader-friendly bimonthly magazine published by Voice International Publications, Inc.

Hearing Health
P.O. Drawer V
Ingleside, TX 78362
(512) 776-7240 (V/TTY)
Website: www.hearinghealthmag.com

The magazine features both first-person stories and articles by staff writers and health professionals.

Volta Voices is a bimonthly magazine available to Alexander Graham Bell Association members. It includes articles about deafness, including education, technology, and advocacy. For information, e-mail to Bell-Member@aol.com or write to the association at the address listed under "Self-Help Groups" above.

Index